I Heart Parenting

I Heart Parenting

Getting the Hearts of Your Children
Before They Break Yours

Dr. H. Wallace Webster

RESOURCE *Publications* · Eugene, Oregon

I HEART PARENTING
Getting the Hearts of Your Children Before They Break Yours

Copyright © 2012 Dr. H. Wallace Webster. All rights reserved. Except for brief quotations in critical publications or reviews, no part of this book may be reproduced in any manner without prior written permission from the publisher. Write: Permissions, Wipf and Stock Publishers, 199 W. 8th Ave., Suite 3, Eugene, OR 97401.

Resource Publications
An Imprint of Wipf and Stock Publishers
199 W. 8th Ave., Suite 3
Eugene, OR 97401
www.wipfandstock.com

ISBN 13: 978-1-62032-536-0
Manufactured in the U.S.A.

All Scripture quotations, unless otherwise indicated, are taken from the King James Version of the Bible (KJV). Public Domain."

Scripture quotations marked NKJV are taken from *The New King James Version*. Copyright © 1982 by Thomas Nelson, Inc. Used by permission. All rights reserved.

Scripture quotations marked NIV are taken from *The Holy Bible: New International Version* ®. NIV. Copyright © 1973, 1978, 1984 by International Bible Society. Used by permission of Zondervan Publishing House. All rights reserved.

Contents

Foreword vii
Dedication and Acknowledgments ix

1 Introduction to the Heart of Parenting 1

Part One: The Importance of the Heart 11

2 Jesus Desires to Have Your Heart 13

3 A Child with a Complete Heart 20

4 Why is the Heart so Important? 29

5 Heart Attacks 36

6 What Kind of Parent Are You? 48

Part Two: The H-E-A-R-T of Parenting 59

7 The "H" Challenge of the Heart—Heart 61

8 The "E" Challenge of the Heart—Entrance 67

9 The "A" Challenge of the Heart—Attitude 75

10 The "R" Challenge of the Heart—Relationships 80

11 The "T" Challenge of the Heart—Training 88

12 From Information to Transformation 103

Part Three: Practical Application 109

13 Some Important Must Do's for the Heart 111

14 FAQs About the Heart of Parenting 132

15 Parenting from a Mom's Perspective 144

16 Help for the Hurting Parent 156

17 A Word to the Children 162

PART FOUR: THE CONCLUSION OF IT ALL 177

18 Leaving a Legacy 179

Afterword 185
Bibliography 187

Foreword

IT IS PROBABLY BEST to begin by asking the question that will be on most people's hearts as they pick up this book: what gives you the right to write a book on parenting? The answer just might surprise you.

Whenever anyone writes a book on any subject, they claim to be some kind of authority and to have a record to demonstrate that they know what they are talking about. Should Derek Jeter write a book on hitting a baseball, most would say he has the right to do so. Should Michael Jordan write a book on shooting a basketball, most would agree that he should have that privilege. Should Steven Spielberg write a book on directing a great movie, I would imagine that many would believe he is qualified. My story is different: I am not writing this book because my children have all turned out perfectly. My children have not turned out perfectly because they are not perfect, and they did not have a perfect example in me or their mother. So, then what gives me the right to author this book?

I am writing this book because after 25 years of parenting, I can truthfully say that I wished I had this book when I began the journey. There are things I did correctly as a parent simply by the grace of God, and I don't believe that experience is the best teacher—unless it is someone else's experience. If I told you that a certain gas station in town was watering down their gas, which would eventually destroy your vehicle, would you brush that off as nonsense and keep on using the gas from that station? Now, if the mechanic who examines your car comes to the same conclusion, would that make any difference? Basically, I am something of an authority on parenting due to the fact that I have learned so many great truths about parenting while making so many mistakes. My children have turned out to be wonderful young people for the cause of Christ, but that is not why I have the right to be the author of this book. I am here to extol the grace and mercy of God and to offer tips and thoughts that I have learned on this grace trip of our parenting experiences and those of others. You only get one life time to impact

Foreword

your children for the cause of the Kingdom, so let's at least examine these ideas to determine their validity.

Congratulations on having the desire to seek deeper enjoyment of parenting! My prayer is that you will gather many nuggets from this parent that will enable you to be a far better parent that I ever was. In this book are some clear guidelines and principles that I believe have helped shape my children into God's servants for His glory. I believe that these are timeless and will work for any family and any situation. But in the end, all glory goes to our Lord and Savior, for if God has used me in any way, it is truly about His grace and mercy. I often say that if I were in the Bible, I would be the lad who had the bag lunch that was offered to Jesus. My part may have been a little different, though: I would have swung the bag so often that the fish and chips would be gone. I would have brought simply an empty, battered, and torn bag to Jesus. Yes, God loves to use those kinds of people (1 Cor 2)! May He alone receive the glory.

Enjoy your journey as a parent, and I pray that when you're finished with those years, you will "heart" parenting as much as we have!

Dedication and Acknowledgments

THIS BOOK IS DEDICATED to the women in my life who have greatly impacted me and helped make me the man I am today. I have been greatly blessed to have a godly heritage as the Timothy of the Bible. He had a godly grandmother and mother and so did I. I would like to dedicate this book to those who first made an impact on me regarding family. There was my grandmother, Irene, who was an amazing example of godliness and holiness. Her prayers still ring loudly in my ears. Then there is my mother, Nora, who is still alive and going strong at age 85. She is a rock solid example to me of what a mother ought to be. I will forever be grateful. Then I want to express my deepest respect to my wife, Vicky, who is truly behind every page of this book. I could not have written this book with these principles without an amazing wife along side of me. She modeled these truths that I write so freely about. I also want to acknowledge my dear Aunt Gert who is undoubtedly my biggest encourager of all time. Everyone ought to have an Aunt Gert that they can call for support 24/7. Lastly, I want to dedicate this book to my four beautiful daughters, Jessica, Jennifer, Kirsten, and Katelyn. I often pinch myself to make sure that I am not living a dream. These four beautiful and wonderful daughters have made it easy for me to be a parent.

I especially want to acknowledge my incredible editor, Heather Bronner. Words cannot express clearly enough my appreciation for all her hard work. Halfway through the project I asked her if maybe we should not be co-authors. She has left her fingerprints all throughout with careful and meticulous edits. Truthfully, much praise for her efforts is a small comment.

I want to send a special note of appreciation to my church family, who gave me the time to write this book. Thank you from the bottom of my heart.

Finally, I want to acknowledge my Lord and Savior Jesus Christ. He alone deserves all the glory because without Him, I can do nothing.

Dedication and Acknowledgments

He gave me the words, the idea, the time, and the strength. He is the reason for life and all that is part of life, including parenting. Without Jesus Christ, I have no meaning, purpose, or identity, and I would be living an aimless life. I look forward to seeing Him one day and casting this work at His feet.

1

Introduction to the Heart of Parenting

STATISTICS DO NOT ALWAYS give a perfect picture of a situation, but they certainly give enough trends so that we can draw conclusions from the details. One such area is the overwhelming information that is available concerning the problems teens face. A brief internet search is very revealing; I found 51 million links to begin my study! Of course, I did not examine every site, but I read enough of them to learn of the plethora of statistics on teen issues and concerns. Let me share some of the statistics from a number of sources that illustrate the fact that something is missing in the parent/child relationship. Many statistics have been published that show the dangers youth face today. Whether their exposure comes through the news, their friends, or just "the grapevine," they learn things that their parents never even considered while they were in school.

Teenage Sexuality Statistics

- Every day, 8,000 teenagers in the United States become infected by a sexually transmitted disease. This year, nearly 3 million teens will become infected. Overall, roughly one-quarter of the nation's sexually active teens have been infected by a sexually transmitted disease (STD).[1]

- When compared to teens that are not sexually active, teenage boys and girls who are sexually active are significantly less likely to be happy and more likely to feel depressed.[2]

---

1. Meg Meeker, *Epidemic: How Teen Sex Is Killing Our Kids* (Washington, D.C.: Lifeline Press, 2002), p. 12.
2. Meeker, p. 13

- When compared to teens that are not sexually active, teenage boys and girls who are sexually active are significantly more likely to attempt suicide.[3]
- 25.3 percent of sexually active teens are depressed vs. 7.7 percent of teens who are not sexually active.[4]
- 14.3 percent of sexually active girls attempted suicide while 5.1 percent of teens who are not sexually active have attempted suicide.[5]
- A study reported in *Pediatrics* magazine found that sexually active boys aged 12 through 16 are four times more likely to smoke and six times more likely to use alcohol than are those who describe themselves as virgins. Among girls in this same age cohort, those who are sexually active are seven times more likely to smoke and 10 times more likely to use marijuana than are those who are virgins.[6]
- Currently 46.8 percent of all high school students report they have had sexual intercourse.[7]
- Nationwide, 6.2 percent of high school students had had sexual intercourse for the first time before age 13. Overall, the prevalence of having had sexual intercourse before age 13 was higher among male (8.8 percent) than female (3.7 percent) students.[8]
- Among the 33.9 percent of currently sexually active high school students nationwide, 23.3 percent had drunk alcohol or used drugs before their last sexual intercourse.[9]
- Youth exposed to sexual content on television were more likely to overestimate the frequency of sexual activity among peers and more likely to have more permissive attitudes toward premarital sex.[10]

    3. Robert Rector, Kirk Johnson, Ph.D., Lauren Noyes, "Sexually Active Teenagers Are more Likely to Be Depressed and to Attempt Suicide," www.heritage.org, June 3, 2003.
    4. National Longitudinal Survey of Adolescent Health, Wave II, 1996.
    5. *Ibid.*
    6. Alan Guttmacher Institute, "Sex and America's Teenagers."
    7. CDC. Youth risk behavior surveillance—United States, 2011. *MMWR* 2012; 61(SS-4).
    8. *Ibid.*
    9. *Ibid.*
    10. "ADD Health." UNC Carolina Population Center. www.cpcunc.edu/projects.addhealth

Introduction to the Heart of Parenting

Teenage Drug Statistics

- The Monitoring Future Survey in 2001 showed that 20 percent of eighth-graders have tried marijuana at least once, and by 10th grade, 20 percent are "current" users (that is, used within the past month). Among 12th-graders, nearly 50 percent have tried marijuana or hash at least once, and about 22 percent were current users.[11]
- Drug use has gone down since 1990 but prescription drug use has skyrocketed among teens since then.[12]
- The risk of using cocaine is estimated to be more than 104 times greater for those who have tried marijuana than for those who have never tried it.[13]

Teenage Obesity and Eating Disorder Statistics

- Childhood obesity has increased in children ages 6–17 from six percent in 1980 to 18 percent in 2004.[14]
- Obesity is one of the leading causes of low self-esteem.[15]
- Obesity often is easily fixed by minor adjustments in a teen's life.[16]
- Eating disorders (specifically anorexia and bulimia) in kids under the age of 12 rose 119 percent over the past nine years. Eating disorders on the whole rose 15 percent.[17]

These are just some of the concerns that we need to be cautioned about, and they should certainly cause parents some thought. Something is going wrong!

11. "At What Age Do Children Generally Start Smoking Pot?", http://alcoholism.about.com, Nov. 22, 2007.

12. Gdcada.org/statistics (The Council on Alcohol & Drug Abuse)

13. *Ibid.*

14. Federal Interagency Forum on Child and Family Statistics. *America's Children: Key National Indicators of Well-Being, 2007.* Federal Interagency Forum on Child and Family Statistics, Washington, DC: U.S. Government Printing Office.

15. *Ibid.*

16. *Ibid.*

17. Therapist Tempe Bureau, "Eating Disorders and Kids: Statistics Show How Little We Know," http://www.GoodTherapy.org, 2010.

While I am not sure that the causes today are really any different than the causes of years gone by, the number of teens who are going astray truly seems to be a great proportion. Even one teen going the wrong direction is one too many, especially when it is your child. And this book is designed to offer some help and encouragement to parents in the process of training up children in the way that they should go. By the way, although these are some general statistics, unfortunately Christian homes face many of the same problems.

Scriptural Warnings

The Bible has much to say about parenting issues, and Scripture is actually rather precise about children going astray. It explains that this is a warning sign to our generation. One central passage is found in 2 Tim 3:1–5:

> But mark this: There will be terrible times in the last days. People will be lovers of themselves, lovers of money, boastful, proud, abusive, *disobedient to their parents*, ungrateful, unholy, without love, unforgiving, slanderous, without self-control, brutal, not lovers of the good, treacherous, rash, conceited, lovers of pleasure rather than lovers of God—having a form of godliness but denying its power. Have nothing to do with such people. [emphasis mine]

Paul's description of the last days could certainly describe today! Notice the many parallels:

1. Lovers of themselves—A quick perusal of any bookstore will reveal that one of the largest sections is on the subject of self. Self-help books are major sellers, and they are available in every conceivable subject. We are a society consumed with self!

2. Lovers of money—Everywhere one turns, the issue of money is forefront of the conversations. Even as this book goes to print we are engaged in a hotly debated political climate where, once again, many claim that the major issue in America is the economy. (I personally do not believe the economy is the major issue, but morality. Nevertheless, lovers of money prevail.)

3. Boastful—Everyone today claims to be number one about something. Even small children will run all over the field claiming to be number one after scoring a goal.

4. Proud—Pride has always been with us, but today humility seems very conspicuous by its absence.

5. Abusive—Hardly a day passes where some form of abuse is not highlighted, frequently in circles where you would least expect it.

6. Disobedient to parents—Now that seems an odd thing to include in such a list as we have in this passage! Paul suggests that we will know we are in the end times when children are basically disobedient to parents. Every generation has had disobedient children. Even in Old Testament Israel, laws were put in place to deal with disobedient children (Deut 21:18–21). So why would Paul put such a "normal" thing in this catalog of sins? I believe it is because there will be a generation known more for its disobedience than for its obedience. (I believe that is true of all of the items in this list. They may have always existed, but not in the magnitude of the end times.) Disobedient children truly are the norm for our day!

7. Ungrateful—Lack of gratitude is characteristic of this generation.

8. Unholy—With the evolution of the internet, children have access to web material that their parents would have had to search diligently for and obtain illicitly. Today, many bring it right into their homes with the touch of a finger! It depicts an unholy generation.

9. Without love—Need I say more?

10. Unforgiving—Asking forgiveness is becoming such an outdated concept that I would venture to say many can't remember the last time someone did anything wrong and asked to be forgiven. Is our generation that good that we don't need forgiveness?

11. Slanderers—Every day it seems like someone is being sued over slander, and often slandering the other guy in the process!

12. Without self control—Is this not part of our obesity problem?

13. Brutal—Just watch any of the movies around Halloween.

14. Not lovers of good—Where have all the morally good television shows gone?

15. Treacherous, rash, conceited—To be sly or snide, to act without thinking, saying, "It doesn't matter what anyone else thinks so long as I am happy"—not an unusual thing!

16. Lovers of pleasure more than lovers of God—People spent $10.22 billion on movies[18] and $74 billion on games in 2011,[19] while just $126 billion was given to religious charities.[20] So, if you add the amount spent on vacations, dining out, and other forms of recreation, Americans alone invest a far greater amount of money into personal pleasures than to God. And the number continues to grow in favor of lovers of pleasure.

The numbers indicate that we are living in a time when rebellion and behavior problems are on the rise. And the definition of insanity, of course, is to continue to do the same things over and over and expect different results. We have to do better and we have to do some things differently.

It's Not all Bad News

I dare not leave this section under such a cloud of discouragement and doomsday thinking. Yes, we are in difficult times. Yes, things do not look good. Yes, in many areas, we are losing the battle, which means we are losing our kids. So, where would the good news come from? God. Keep the following firmly in mind:

Conception is the work of God. Man and woman may come together biologically and perform the necessary actions to put in motion the "baby production" process, but conception is, without question, the work of God. Scripture makes it clear in many places, but the best might be Psalm 139. Just a quick perusal of verses 13–17 will clearly portray the work of God in "creating" a child in the mother's womb:

> For You formed my inward parts;
> You covered me in my mother's womb.
> I will praise You, for I am fearfully *and* wonderfully made;
> Marvelous are Your works,
> And *that* my soul knows very well.

---

18. Associated Press, "Movie Ticket Sales Fell Sharply in 2011," www.cbsnews.com, 2 Jan. 2012.

19. Anand Rai, "Money Spent on Gaming to Reach $112 Billion in 2015: Gartner," http://techcircle.vccircle.com, 6 July, 2011.

20. Joshua Bolding, "Church Donations Growing at Less than Half the Rate of Overall Charitable Giving," *Deseret News*, 20 Jan. 2012.

Introduction to the Heart of Parenting

> My frame was not hidden from You,
> When I was made in secret,
> *And* skillfully wrought in the lowest parts of the earth.
> Your eyes saw my substance, being yet unformed.
> And in Your book they all were written,
> The days fashioned for me,
> When *as yet there were* none of them.
> How precious also are Your thoughts to me, O God!
> How great is the sum of them! (NKJV)

We also know that it is even possible for God to "produce" a person without a man or woman coming together. Scripture gives at least three lives to demonstrate this for us. One, God made Adam from the dust of the ground (Gen 2:7); two, He made Eve from Adam's side (Gen 2:18–22); and three, He "made" the baby Jesus by the Holy Spirit (Matt 1:18). God makes babies, and we need to make sure we understand that from the beginning in our parenting. Therefore, he has a vested interest in every child, even if that child is not where they need to be spiritually!

Children are a gift from God (Psalm 127:3). Every child that has ever been conceived has been a personal gift from God to mankind. Often when the abortion issue is debated, the first line of argument is that the woman ought to have the right over her body. Unfortunately, it is not such a simple issue.

The first line of argument needs to be the "right" of God. He is carefully making this baby and ought to have the say in his or her future. Additionally, not only the couple, but an entire civilization can be impacted by one single life. Just think of all the differences that one person can make in a lifetime! Think of the gifts of Albert Einstein, Benjamin Franklin, George Washington, Winston Churchill, Martin Luther King, and so many others. What if that generation and their parents had not seen the value of a child? Conception and children need to be seen in a larger context than simply the mother and father. Children are a gift from God to the world which they will enter, and every person who enters this world ought to make the world a better place because of their presence. Of course, not everyone will be a prodigy or a genius, but that does not take away from the potential God has put in motion. Parents get to help mold that child for the journey already set in motion for them by God. We don't need to invent the path, just help our children understand their path and guide them accordingly. What an awesome privilege and responsibility!

God loves these children more than we do. On numerous occasions when God's Son was on this earth, He picked up little children and held them in His arms (Mark 10:13–16). Scripture also says that God is the Father to the fatherless (Psalm 68:5), and we are strongly encouraged to visit the orphan as a model of pure religion (James 1:27). Not a tear falls on a pillow at night that our sleepless Heavenly Father does not notice. We can be sure that He does not want our children into drugs, on the streets, in broken homes, or dealing with any of the myriad of other problems that they often encounter. The fact that they do experience these pains does not negate God's care for them. We live in a fallen world with evil all around; the rain falls on the just and unjust. Yet God will be the Avenger of those who harm children.

God knows how to reach every child in any situation that they may encounter. You may be experiencing personally a difficult situation that no one seems to understand how to resolve. There are no such situations with God. We serve the God of the impossible, and although the situation may look bleak, and the statistics may not be in your favor, you need to be directed to look up where our hope is found (Psalm 121:1–2). Remember that although we may lose some battles, the last chapter of the Bible reminds us that we are going to win the war! We can confidently claim our children by the grace and mercy of God that not one of them will be lost.

The devil does not have all the children. Even though 2 Timothy says that children will be disobedient to parents, and even though we see much of that in place today, there are still rays of hope in many communities where kids are doing great things and making a difference. Not all kids are rebellious, and not all teens are troubled. There are some good things going on in parenting. I have personally been involved with youth for over 40 years, and I have seen many teens on fire for God. Read on with optimism that "greater is He that is in you, than he that is in the world" (1 John 4:4).

God takes no pleasure in broken lives and broken homes. Even though these exist, we should not assume that they are God's will or God's desire or God's best. When Adam and Eve sinned in the Garden, there were many consequences. Broken homes and broken lives are just two results of a fallen world, and good people feel the effects of the judgment of those around them. Just like one believer can have a sanctifying effect on a household (I Cor 7:14), so also may one non-believer

Introduction to the Heart of Parenting

or one rebellious person disrupt the good. Just ask any family who has one wayward individual in their home; the effects are sometimes too overwhelming to imagine. God does not desire that for His children. His thoughts towards us are good (Jer 29:11), and "Who shall lay anything against God's elect?" (Rom 8:33). God is for us and for our families, but there may be pain in that pathway. Never lose hope that God cares and only wants the best for us (Rom 8:28), even if we are unable to see it at the time. Could a rebellious child be part of God's plan? While He doesn't cause the rebellion, He can take that which is done in rebellion and produce good. Just ask Joseph and his brothers in Genesis 37–50. Especially note 50:20: "What you meant for evil, God intended for good."

God's Word will not return without doing what it was intended to do (Is 55:11). That is why it is so important to saturate your children with the Word of God. They cannot get too much of the Scriptures. Too often, parents choose to skip Sunday school or other avenues of spiritual training for their children, fearing that too much will cause them to walk away. Instead, these well-meaning parents give their kids more sports, television, or similar things which pull them away from the Lord. Additionally, many parents let their children choose how much spiritual training they should receive. Let me make it clear: spiritual decisions should *not* be left in the hands of your children. Very few would ever go to Sunday school on their own or choose a Christian school if they have friends in public school. You don't let your kids pick their medical care, do you? If you don't let them choose something which has only medical impact, why would you let them choose something that has eternal impact? Be the parent and saturate your child with Scripture, and then watch the power of Scripture change their lives. (More on this in later chapters.)

Let me illustrate this with a personal example. During my sophomore year of Bible college, I began to have regular quiet time with the Lord. I had seen many of the upperclassmen reading their Bibles, so I thought that since I was a sophomore, I should do as they did. I went to the chapel and rarely missed a day. My motives were all wrong, and I went into the Word for selfish gain. God, however, used the daily immersion in the Word to change my heart. The impact it made on me during my second year of college may very well have changed my entire life. Don't underestimate the power of saturating your children with

Scripture. They can run but they cannot hide. And on a funny note, they will learn it so well that they will begin to give it back to you! It's not a bad bit of motivation for parents to live what they preach.

As I close this chapter, let me reiterate the encouragement of Scripture that God is on the side of righteousness. Never underestimate the power of prayer, Scripture, church, godly environments, and whatever else you can use to help mold your children. It does not take a village to raise a child, but it does take God, and He has a good plan for these children. Never doubt what our God is capable of doing!

Part One

The Importance of the Heart

If you see a red light on the dashboard of your car, you know you have to take action before something critical happens. If you ignore it, you risk finding yourself on the side of the road. Similarly, if you don't realize that the heart is important, you may not take action and find yourself sitting on the side of the bed wondering where things got off track in your child's life.

2

Jesus Desires to Have Your Heart

BEFORE WE ADDRESS His desire for the child's heart, let's make sure we understand that Christianity is not just a simple story that pertains to children. Jesus and children often go together to such a degree that parents choose to miss out. Parents believe it is important to get their children to church, get them baptized, and give them some religious training, and I agree. The children's favorite song typically is "Jesus Loves the Little Children," and He does. But it does not stop there. Jesus also loves their parents, and parents need to hear His call to them, as well! It is often the parents' example that lights the match of faith in the children's hearts.

More is Caught than Taught

Parents too often want their children to do something that they won't do. This book will explain how important it is for the heart of the child to be turned toward God. But wouldn't it be helpful for that child to have parents whose hearts are also turned toward God? And wouldn't it be a detriment for the parents to ignore God but expect the child to give Him full attention?

I have observed many parents who want a "little Jesus" for their kids, but they don't see any need for Jesus themselves. They see the need for little Johnnie to go to Sunday school, but they don't see their own need. They believe their child should to go to youth retreats, but they never go to adult or family retreats. They want their child to read the Bible, but they never read it themselves.

The battle for your child's heart really begins with a battle for your hearts, parents. How do expect your child to get what you don't have and are not modeling for them? There is a picture on the wall at the recruitment office that portrays Uncle Sam pointing his finger at the viewer and saying, "I Want You," and you could easily see our Savior saying the same thing. As much as this is a book about the children, I also desire that this message would lodge deep in the parents' hearts. Let God have your heart, dear parent, and help your children follow.

Going After Dad

Children who grow up in homes where dad is a man after God's own heart have a far greater chance to gain a like mindset. Dads have been so neglected over the years that many of them have become AWOL to the cause of Christ. There is no room for deadbeat dads when it comes to parenting. Dear ladies, please ask your husband to read the following sections. Dear dads, please take the time to look over these thoughts. The worst that could happen is that you will spend about half an hour of your time reading.

As a dad, I can certainly understand the struggles and trials that go with being a man in this era. We have lost the era of *Father Knows Best* and have slid into the time of "Dad is stupid." When dads are not in their rightful place, the family often drifts far away from God.

First, you need to realize your need for the Savior. Too many men think that they can do it all by themselves, but Scripture says just the opposite. Read carefully the following:

- Romans 3:10—There is none righteous, no not one.
- Romans 3:23—For all have sinned and come short of the glory of God.
- Romans 5:12—Wherefore as by one man [Adam], sin entered the world, and death by sin, and so death passed upon all men, for all have sinned.
- Romans 6:23—For the wages of sin is death, but the gift of God is eternal life through Jesus Christ, our Lord.

These verses explain that mankind is in trouble, including dads. God has a high standard of perfection, and no one can measure up. As a matter of fact, everyone who has ever been born stands in direct opposition to God—all because of inherited sin. When Adam, the first person who lived, sinned, so did everyone else. He acted as our representative

(Adam = man), and man chose to sin. Consequently, everyone is born with sin inherited from Adam, and as a result, every person must die. Men, you may think you have it all together, and you may think you don't need Jesus, but the opposite is actually true. You need Jesus because He is the only One who can take away your sin, and you need Jesus because you cannot be the best parent possible without Him. Going after the heart of your child when God does not have your heart is hypocritical. Going after your child begins with your submission to the One who has been after you since birth; does He have your heart? You see, Jesus came to die for the sins of the world:

- John 1:29—"Behold the Lamb of God [Jesus] who takes away the sin of the world."
- John 3:16—"For God so loved the world [the people] that He gave His only Begotten Son that whosoever believes on Him shall not perish, but have everlasting life."

Jesus' mission on earth was to seek and save the lost (Luke 19:10). He went to the cross to die for the sins of every man who ever lived, and as He hung dying there, He cried out: "It is finished!" (John 19:30). In other words, "I have done what I came to do. I have paid for the sins of all mankind, and My Father has accepted the payment in full. Now whoever believes in Me shall have life and have it forever."

Everybody who has ever lived on this earth has had one of two masters. Either he is the master of his life, or he has turned that life over to Jesus' mastery. It is as if there is a throne in your heart. When you are born, you crawl up on that seat and claim authority over your life and destiny. You continue on that path until you die, unless you have an encounter with Jesus, which Scripture calls being "born again." Without this, you will end up separated from Jesus forever throughout eternity. Not only do you miss out on this life, but you will miss out on the life to come! This is not a decision that you should take lightly. Examine the Scriptures and make sure you understand the gravity of sin and consequences before a holy God.

So how does one become a follower of Jesus? It is actually simple enough for a child. First, let me make sure you understand what it is not:

1. It is not being baptized.
2. It is not going to church.

I Heart Parenting

3. It is not giving money.
4. It is not becoming a member.
5. It is not doing good works.

Although these are all very good things, and every Christian ought to do them, just works alone will not save you. Ephesians 2:8–9 makes it clear: "For by grace are you saved through faith; and that not of yourselves, it is the gift of God. Not of works, lest any man should boast." If doing something could save you from your sin and get you into Heaven, then Jesus came for nothing. Please let me make this clear: you were born separated from God, and if you were truly honest with yourself, you would admit it. There is a void in you that only God is big enough to fill. Men try to fill it with all kinds of things: pleasures, hobbies, thrills, and a host of different options. But these only satisfy temporarily. After that rush is over, you will need another fix of some sort to satisfy, and often the drive is for greater and bigger. Until you find your peace with God, you are not going to have any peace on this earth. Are you ready for God to have His rightful place as Lord of your life, sitting on the throne of your heart? If so, it is rather simple. Here is what you need to pray:

1. Recognize that you are a sinner and have sinned and are separate from God.
2. Recognize that you cannot fix your situation, and you are in need of a Savior.
3. Recognize that Jesus is that Savior.
4. Ask Him to come into your life and forgive your sin and sit on the throne of your life and lead your life.
5. Declare Him as Lord of your life and confess Him as Savior.

If you have just prayed this prayer with these thoughts, then Scripture says you are saved. Romans 10:9–10 reads: "That if you shall confess with your mouth the Lord Jesus and believe in your heart that God has raised Him from the dead, you shall be saved. For with the heart man believes unto righteousness, and with the mouth confession is made unto salvation." Your salvation is guaranteed. No one can take it away.

Now that you are a believer in Jesus, and now that He has your heart, you are more equipped to go after the hearts of your children

Jesus Desires to Have Your Heart

for His honor and glory. Giving your heart to Jesus is the path God has ordered for your family. Now go and lead them down the path towards righteousness.

Perhaps you are thinking, "But I'm fine. I accepted Jesus as my Savior years ago! I follow Him." That is exciting, but let me probe that a little deeper. What do you mean by that? If you could see that throne on your heart, would you see that God is truly the King of your life? Do you live daily to give Him the glory as much as possible, and do you do everything for Him? Or are you playing at being a Christian? Here are some things that ought to be true of you if you claim to be a follower of Jesus. Can you say:

1. I attend church faithfully?
2. I read the Word regularly (mostly daily)?
3. I pray consistently?
4. I am a good testimony for Jesus and all friends know I am a Christian?
5. I have no bad behaviors that dishonor God?
6. My family knows I love Jesus?
7. The pastor of my church can count on me as a faithful brother in the Lord?

In other words, if you were to stand before a court of law, on trial for being a Christian, would there be enough evidence to convict you? If these things aren't true in your life, maybe you are just playing at being a Christian. You may talk the talk, but you are not walking the walk. There are two possible scenarios here. One is that you are a Christian but have slipped away from a genuine walk. If that is so, you need to repent and get right with God. Your children notice your hypocrisy, and you are a detriment to their growth in Christ. You cannot lead your family where you personally are not going. The other possibility is that you are not a Christian at all. Judas Iscariot followed Jesus for three years, and as best as the other eleven could tell, he was the real deal. Even when he left on the night of the betrayal to plot Jesus' arrest with the religious leaders, none of the disciples suspected anything. He was able to fool his closest friends, but of course, he never fooled Jesus. Maybe you need to go back to the earlier section and pray the sinner's prayer and stop playing the game. Not only does your soul depend on this, so might the souls of your children. The greatest thing you can give your children is Jesus, and you cannot give to them what you personally do not have.

Jesus came to be the Savior and Lord of every person, and it is all about the heart. On one occasion, a man asked Jesus what the greatest commandment in the Law was. Jesus responded without any hesitation: "You shall love the Lord your God with all your *heart*, soul, mind, and strength" (Matt 22:37). Notice the very first thing to love God with—all your heart. Fathers—and mothers—surrender your hearts to the Lord so you can model it for your children and lead them to surrender their hearts to Him.

How to Lead Your Child to Jesus

I cannot think of a more important process in parenting than leading your children to a salvation experience with Jesus. Even though they are precious, they are still in need of a Savior. Everything a parent does must have the goal of bringing the child to Jesus. You want it to be genuine, so you don't want to force them into salvation, but you must do all you can to provide the correct environment for the child to become a follower of Jesus.

Here are some of the keys to that process. Realize that God can still save even if all of these are not in place. He is the Savior, but it certainly does not hurt to provide the scenario that best supports the salvation experience.

1. Regularly saturate your family with Jesus, using Bible reading, church, Christian videos and music, and whatever you can discover for your family. I am not suggesting that they cannot watch a harmless secular video, but your goal remember is not entertainment, but transformation.

2. Talk with them often about Jesus. Give them the brief facts that line up theologically with Scripture. Jesus is God's Son, and He came to earth to love us and give us salvation. As they grow older, the Gospel can become more defined, although the horror of the cross must be given to them age-appropriately.

3. They need to be taught that they sin because they are sinners. When a child does wrong, it is certainly right to let them know that they have disobeyed Mom, Dad, and Jesus, and that is called sin. Children certainly respond well to Jesus as they should, and bringing their gaze to Jesus regularly is the right approach. Let them know that He does not want sin in their lives.

4. Once they are of the age to understand all the correct Biblical doctrines for salvation, then look for the time when they might be ready to give their heart to Jesus. What a great joy for a parent to introduce their child to Christ. There might not be any greater joy (3 John 4)!

5. After they pray the prayer, then begin to disciple them in their walk. Give them Bible study helps, teach them to pray, and help them on their journey. Disciple making begins at home.

Guiding your children to faith in Christ and helping them grow in this faith is not going to make them perfect, but it will certainly help them with their obedience and actions. Otherwise you are trying to force Christian actions on a non-Christian, and that simply will not work. It only makes for legalism and bondage. The heart must be changed for the truths to make a long-lasting impact.

3

A Child with a Complete Heart

IF YOU WERE TOLD to paint a sunset, you might sit for many evenings and watch the Master Painter do His work, and then you would imitate some of those breathtaking elements you see on your canvas. What if you had a model child placed in front of you that you could emulate, one that you could have your children see and re-create in their own lives?

I have great news for you! We have such a Child, and His name is Jesus. Although we only know about small portions of His childhood, we actually have enough to use as a model, and it is all summarized in two verses by Dr. Luke. Jesus was 12 years old at the time this incident occurred, but the verses give us a hint of how he grew up in a home that was truly centered on correct parenting standards. They are a great start for our parenting process. Luke 2:51–52 says: "And he went down with them, and came to Nazareth, and was subject unto them: but his mother kept all these sayings in her heart. And Jesus increased in wisdom and stature, and in favour with God and man." These verses suggest four important areas of Jesus' childhood training by His earthly parents, Joseph and Mary:

1. Jesus increased in wisdom – that is the intellectual.
2. Jesus increased in stature – that is the physical.
3. Jesus increased in favor with God – that is the spiritual.
4. Jesus increased in favor with man – that is the social.

These four facets help comprise a completed young person. It would seem logical to suggest that if you could raise your children to excel in these areas, then truly your children would be as well balanced as

A Child with a Complete Heart

Jesus was. It would also be true that if any of these four areas is out of balance, the child would be out of balance. Let's look at these concepts a little further. They are not listed in any particular order; wisdom is first simply because one needed to be listed first.

Jesus Increased in Wisdom—Intellectual

Wisdom would encompass the area of the intellect, or the learning process of the child. Surely any parent would want their child to be intellectually competent!

Over the years, I have been amazed at the comments parents make about their children. I have heard things like: "She is already speaking in sentences," "He picks up things so quickly," "Her memory is amazing!" The list goes on and on. I find it fascinating that I never hear things like: "My child is developing slowly; he may be the dumbest kid in nursery," or something like that. It appears that every parent is producing some kind of intellectual giant. And just imagine, parents who aren't particularly intellectual produced children of such deep abilities! Needless to say, it is not long before the truth surfaces! (That is, unless the parents are in some kind of denial and they just determine their little Einstein is just not applying himself.)

One thing is certain: children need to be developed intellectually. Much care should be put into positioning your child in the best intellectual development path. That may not mean the same thing for each family; it is not wise to assume your educational process is the same for everyone else. Each child is made in the image of God, and He made no exact replicas. Each child has his own specific DNA, and only God knows what will make him develop intellectually. That is why educational decisions need to be made prayerfully. There may be even cases where the path of each child in a family may be different. Families should not assume that the path that is best for the oldest child is the same path for all the rest. Pray about it!

First, understand that intellectual development begins before kindergarten. Do not assume that the first five years are simply wasted years. Children are beginning to form habits and learning even before they are born. Doctors continue to confirm that babies begin to learn in the womb (Yes, they are babies, not fetuses).

Those early years are a good time to begin the saturation process. We are quick to put our children in front of *Sesame Street* or another secular teaching device (which by itself may not be bad), but also examine all that is out there from the Christian community, such as *Donut Man*, *Veggie Tales*, and *Patch the Pirate*. I would also suggest reading Bible stories to them as you tuck them in at night. Begin to acquire Christian books of all kinds, and regularly read them to your children throughout the day. The 10 minutes it takes to read some of them will begin to set a strong foundation for biblical thirst. I remember reading the *Chronicles of Narnia* series to one of our daughters while she was only an infant. How much did she truly comprehend? Maybe not all of it, but the issue is intentional saturation, which makes a difference in time.

While those years continue, the next area of concern is the formal education that you will choose for your children. This is *not* the child's decision. I have frequently heard how parents allow their children to determine the educational process themselves. Really? You leave the choice of education up to your child? "Well," you may say, "I don't want my child to resent my decisions for them!" Get used to it, parents. You are not parenting to please your children, but to please God. Letting your children decide their educational direction is shirking your duty.

Jesus' home would have been one of proper intellectual stimulation. If you don't believe it, just take a look at Him at age 12 when He is in the temple dialoguing with doctors and lawyers about the Law. How many 12-year-olds do you know who can carry on an intellectual conversation with adults? Remember that Jesus is our Model. So, ask yourself this question: if you were Jesus' parents today, where would you send Jesus to school? Making educational decisions for your children is just as serious, so make them with time and prayer.

Jesus Increased in Stature—Physical

Today's children are basically out of shape and overweight. Physical education that once was part of all curriculums now is difficult to find in many schools. Additionally, poor eating and sleeping habits, too much television, and too much time in front of a computer and electronic games generate children with a lack of desire for proper physical exercise. Parents are often at fault: they put games and electronics and televisions in their children's rooms so the children will stay out of their hair. Unfortunately, few children are going to push themselves in the area of physical exercise—it needs to be a monitored activity. Do you watch what your children are doing? Additionally, are you sure your children are getting enough rest? Are they eating enough calories every day and getting a balanced diet?

Jesus had a major task in front of Him, and if you read about the last days of His life on earth, you will see that He was physically fit. I am not suggesting that He was a body builder, but very few could have endured what He had to face physically without being very fit indeed! How was He able to bear up under all the pain and torture He was given? At least one primary reason is that He was in great condition physically. He did not neglect the importance of being physically fit—nor should we. One reason parents disregard this area is because they themselves are not physically fit. We need to remember that our bodies are the temples of God; we should make as much effort as our children to stay fit. We never know when God may call us to do something that requires stamina and endurance. How sad to miss out because we are unable to complete whatever God may want us to do!

Do not leave this up to your children to discover or decide. Parents are responsible for the physical well-being of their children. They need proper pre-natal care (diet, rest, fluids, etc.), and they need proper post-natal care. Most parents are so careful about the baby in the womb. Moms eat so carefully, take vitamins, even exercise. They visit doctors frequently, and should there appear to be some kind of problem, they spare no expense on tests. The baby must be healthy and have ten toes and ten fingers. I commend parents for this diligent care, but why should it stop once the baby is born? Shouldn't you give the same conscientious care during the early years, school years, and whatever other years they may be part of your family?

There is another side that too often surfaces in this area: physical overstimulation. I am not sure what drives some parents to go too far, but this is just as dangerous as lack of physical development. Children need controlled and well thought out physical exercise. Yet, sports have become the god of some families; sadly, this happens to good Christian families. Maybe Dad is living out his life in his son. Maybe Mom is trying to be the one who can brag at the club. Maybe it is all about keeping up with the neighbors. Parents need to be very careful in this area. If your children are growing up with a greater knowledge of sports and teams than they are about the intellectual and spiritual, your child is getting out of balance. Many parents today wonder why their child has so little appetite for God, and yet that is what they have helped develop. They miss church regularly for sports. They can never attend Sunday school or youth events for sports. They can be seen more often with a ball or stick or glove in their hands than the Scriptures, and then they have little appetite for spiritual things. The parents have produced a child whose god is sports.

Remember that the physical is just one of four areas of proper development. Any one of these areas can be out of balance, and you need to take care as parents to keep a proper handle on balancing your child and his development. Be the parent and guardian of your child.

I would imagine that growing up in a carpenter's home gave Jesus many opportunities to develop physically. Most carpenters I know are rather physically fit. Handling hammers and lumber is not easy work! Jesus would have kept Himself in great physical condition, and remember that He is our Model!

Jesus Increased in Favor with God—Spiritual

You can learn a lot about a person's childhood by examining their adult life. So when you examine the life of Christ as an adult, you can get a glimpse into His childhood. One such area is His knowledge of Scripture. It is far too easy to say that because Jesus was God, He knew all the things that He talked of as an adult. But I beg to differ. Jesus grew in the spiritual arena just as He had to grow in all the other areas. Hebrews 5:8 even states that He learned obedience. Jesus placed Himself under His parents' authority and learned at their feet. In that day it was not uncommon to have a schoolmaster that was assigned spiritual tutoring of the child. We don't know if Jesus had such a teacher, but by reading about his adult works, we can see that His knowledge of the Old Testament Scriptures was incredible. His brothers, James and Jude, showed the same education in their writings. Joseph and Mary would have taken the Old Testament command literally (Deuteronomy 6), and would have taught their Son while He was sitting down, while He standing up, and whenever the opportunity arose. Jesus was taught to be a spiritual-thinking Child.

A Child with a Complete Heart

How are you making sure your child is learning spiritually? There are three major areas in which a child can grow spiritually: home, church, and school. When these three institutions are all working together with the same goals and same agenda, the potential for spiritual saturation is high. When these three are not in harmony, parents must carefully compensate for the weak areas. For example: you may have a divided home. Either Dad or Mom may not have a spiritual desire. Does that mean the child does not stand a chance to be a spiritual person? Absolutely not. It just means that the believing parent has more to do to ensure the spiritual growth of the child. More care and more intention must be put into the process than if both parents were on the same page spiritually. It is not an impossible task; it will just take a more concerted effort. The same goes with the church or school. You may choose public education for your children. If that is what God desires for your child, then that is what you must do. But you would be foolish to think that your child is going to receive the same spiritual training as a child who is home schooled with a Christian emphasis or attends a true Christian school. You must make sure that you are doing all you can to compensate. Watch your children. Are they growing spiritually? Do you see their hunger for God increasing? Do you see their spiritual vision maturing? If not, you may need to move them out of public education or become more intentional about their spiritual life. It only takes a short time for them to move in a godless direction.

In the area of the church, far too many parents are underutilizing the great benefits of a strong, Christ-centered church. If the pastor is a man of God, keep them in church every Sunday to hear from God. If the Sunday school teachers are spirit-filled teachers, don't let them miss out on Sunday school. Also, if the church has other youth-related ministries such as Junior Church, AWANA, youth groups, etc., do all you can to provide the opportunity for your children to be a part of these spiritual helps. If your church does not have a great program to enhance your children's spiritual growth (notice spiritual is the emphasis here), then you may need to make a decision. As with education, you may have to personally fill the void through other means, or you may have to choose another church for your family. I personally believe that leaving a church for the sake of the children is often a bad idea, but if there is no way to supplement the spiritual area, and you are not receiving any church support in this, then you may need to move on.

Leaving a church is a serious decision. I believe it would be wise to sit down with the leadership of the church and first express your concerns. However, you don't want to lose your children spiritually for the sake of staying at a church. You need to make sure that your children are growing spiritually and can handle Scripture properly. Ultimately this is the responsibility of the parents, but it is certainly acceptable to utilize any resources that might be available to the family, and the church ought to be a great resource.

Jesus was submissive to His Heavenly Father. He had a great spiritual walk, which is evidenced by how He lived out His early years and adult years. Do everything you can to increase your children's spiritual walk.

One question that often surfaces pertains to the area of being out of balance. Is it possible to have too much spiritual stimulation for the child? Well, I do believe that balance is needed in this area as with all the other areas. However, I have yet to meet someone that is so heavenly minded that they are no earthly good. Instead, I have observed that many have the opposite problem: they are so earthly-minded (Romans 12:1-2 – squeezed into the world's mold), that they are no heavenly good. With that said, I don't believe a child needs to read the Scriptures 24/7 or be in church 24/7, etc. No parent lives that kind of life, and even Jesus did not live that kind of life. Balance again is the key, but don't worry about spiritual overstimulation; it probably won't happen. Raise spiritually-minded children for eternal values.

Jesus Increased in Favor with Man—Social

Most families would think that they are doing a good job in the area of social development because they are allowing their children to either have friends, go over to a friend's house, or have friends over. But social development needs to be as intentional as the other areas. Unfortunately, some parents are too trusting in the areas of friendships. Just providing opportunities for friendships does not mean that the child is developing properly in the social arena. While it is true that some kids are just more social than others, it is important not to let their weakness prevent them from developing socially.

Far too many families are on the extreme ends of this spectrum. They either allow their children to run amuck with no concerns about their whereabouts, or they shelter their kids so much that the poor young people cannot even carry on a conversation with anyone. If any adult speaks to the child, they hide under Mom or Dad's coat. There needs to be an emphasis on polite interaction with adults while you teach them discernment with strangers or those who could harm them.

Social development must purposely be taught in the home; parents much teach respect without falling into child abuse and neglect, and polite interaction without tending toward a child-centered philosophy. The pendulum today has swung far toward that latter philosophy. I recall one mom who, at a dinner given by a friend, asked for dark meat. The reason she gave was "I had never had white meat." Thinking it strange, the host probed deeper to try to understand this mom's story. It went as follows: when she was a child, her parents ate the white meat and gave the children the rest, which was usually the dark meat. When she became a mom, she reversed the order and gave the kids the white meat, and she ate what was left over, which was the dark meat. Hence, this mom had never had white meat.

Now what meat a parent may choose to eat is hardly the issue. What this mom exposed was the real issue: child-centered thinking. Her children were in charge of even this small issue in her home. This kind of social development has long-lasting negative consequences. Children begin to see life through their eyes and their agenda. If they don't learn to properly interact within the home, where strong relationships are formed, they will have no idea how to interact in a world that demands respect.

Social development needs to have the proper balance as with all the other areas. Children need to be taught to interact correctly with siblings, relatives, and friends. They also need to be taught their proper place in the home. Children should not be allowed to interrupt parents unless it is an emergency. Additionally, they must not be permitted the control of the home. Children will pit parent against parent and will win. Moms and Dads need to stand together in the development of the child.

Jesus grew up socially developed. He could speak to adults with respect. He knew how to submit to Mom and Dad. He knew how to be the older brother in a family. And although His siblings did not believe in Him at first (John 7:5), they later did come to faith. This might not have been possible had Jesus not properly understood His role in the home.

A Child with a Complete Heart

I have tried to explain Jesus' development from what we have been given in the New Testament. Although there is not a lot of material, it certainly gives us something to build upon. Jesus was the complete Child, and we know the four areas that His parents prioritized for Him. If any parent today would get these four areas in balance, I believe the child will respond with a God-centered, Biblical path. Realize that every child has his own free will, and there are no perfect formulas for parental success. Nevertheless, using Jesus as a Model can certainly lead a family in the best possible direction—developing a child with a complete heart.

4

Why is the Heart so Important?

I AM CONVINCED THAT the heart of the child is the target for every parent. If you have the heart of your child, you can be more instrumental in directing the paths that they take. They will be more open to your counsel, your advice, and your expectations. Without the heart of the child, you are simply attempting to control him or her from the exterior. It is like the example I heard years ago about a child that wanted to stand up in his high chair at the dinner table. It was an ongoing battle for the parents; he adamantly refused to sit down. Finally, Dad had had enough, and he took his strong arm and held the child down during dinner. The response from the child was clear: "I'm sitting down on the outside, but I am standing up on the inside!" Unfortunately, many parents have children in this condition. As long as the parents are physically (strength) and geographically (living at home) able, they have a strong arm on their child's shoulder and the child is submissive. But once the child is out from under Dad's strong arm, he or she rebels. The problem is not as it appears so often. Parents will say, "I don't understand. My child was so compliant when he was at home. I don't understand why he is so rebellious now. I never saw it coming." They never saw it coming because they did not understand an important concept of parenting. Parenting is not controlling, because you can only control when you have leverage. Once the leverage is gone, so is the control. Parenting is about the heart!

Parents use all kinds of leverage to control their kids. In the early years, it might be spanking or keeping something away from them, or time out. Now, these forms of discipline are not wrong in and of themselves (as long as they are not abusive). But the purpose of discipline should not be to conform the child to your will. The purpose of discipline must be to draw the heart to your authority and God's guidance.

We will look at just how to do that in the following chapters. For now, let me address from Scripture the importance of the heart.

The Old Testament and the Heart

In these two sections, I will give many Scripture verses. The heart is the key to all parenting, and, as we see in Scripture, the key to all life. Both the Old Testament and the New Testament address its importance. However, no illustration pictures it better than that of the little girl sitting in the doctor's office. The kind and conscientious doctor, who was very good with children, listened to her heart through his stethoscope. After a moment, he gasped, "I hear someone in your heart!" The girl's eyes got very big as the doctor continued, "I hear a voice! I think it sounds like Barney!" (Barney is a children's television character.)

Her reply is classic; she didn't miss a beat. "Oh no, Doctor. That is not Barney. That is Jesus! Barney is on my underpants."

This girl got it. She understood the importance of having Jesus in your heart. And that is paramount to the parenting process for any family. Let's look at some Scripture:

1. Genesis 6:5—Man is judged by his *heart*.
2. Genesis 6:6—God uses the word *heart* to describe how He is grieved with man.
3. Genesis 8:21—God again uses *heart* to describe His innermost emotions.
4. Genesis 42:28—Joseph's brothers are under conviction about their previous deceptive behavior and the text says that their *hearts* "failed them." In other words, they are despondent.
5. Genesis 45:26—When Jacob is told that Joseph still lives, his *heart* faints (meaning he is overwhelmed with emotions).
6. Exodus 4:21—From this verse and throughout Exodus, Moses mentions that Pharaoh has his *heart* hardened, meaning that he is under God's control. The key component God utilizes to picture this is the heart. The text also later adds that Pharaoh even hardens his own heart.

Why is the Heart so Important?

7. Exodus 28:29-30—Aaron has the breastplate of judgment over his *heart*, suggesting that he is to be guided by his heart.
8. Exodus 35:5—Offerings to God are to be made from a willing *heart*.
9. Leviticus 19:17—This states that we are not to hate someone in our *heart*.
10. Deuteronomy 4:29—This verse forms the foundation of what we will look at later in the New Testament. God tells His people that they are to *seek Him with all their heart*. This phrase is repeated often in the Old Testament.
11. Joshua 5:1—When God's people cross the Jordan, the word circulates throughout the area and the people in the land lose *heart*.
12. Judges 16:17—Samson exposes his *heart* to Delilah.
13. I Samuel 1:8—When Hannah cannot bear a child, her *heart* grieves.
14. I Samuel 10:9—Saul is given another *heart* so he could be king.
15. I Samuel 13:14—When Saul is to be replaced as king, God seeks a man after His own *heart*.
16. I Samuel 16:7 (a vital Old Testament verse on the heart)—God cautions Samuel to avoid looking on the outward to determine the next king. *"Man looks on the outward appearance, but God looks on the heart."*
17. I Kings 8:17-18—All the kings of Judah would be measured by the *heart* of David, their father.
18. The Psalms are full of verses which address the heart.
    a. 4:4—We are to commune with our *heart* on our bed.
    b. 9:1—We are to praise God with our whole *heart*.
    c. 37:4—God will give us the desires of our *heart*.
    d. 51:10—David asks for a clean *heart*.
    e. 62:8—We are to pour out our *heart* before God.
    f. 66:18—God will not hear our prayers if we regard iniquity in our *heart*.
    g. In Psalms alone, the heart is mentioned at least 124 times!

19. Proverbs also mentions it at least 84 times in a much smaller portion of Scripture.

    a. 2:2—"Apply thy *heart* to understanding."

    b. 3:5—"Trust in the Lord with all thy *heart*..."

    c. 4:23—"Keep thy *heart* with all diligence for out of it are the issues of life." This proverb might very well explain the importance of the heart most clearly.

20. Isaiah also has much to say about the heart.

    d. 14:13—It was the seat of Satan's fall.

    e. 29:13—It was how God measured the relationship He had with His people. ("They draw near with their lips but have removed their *heart* from Me.")

This is just the tip of the iceberg of information on the heart! As best as I could count, there are about 724 mentions of the heart in the Old Testament!

Now what does all this mean? Well, any serious student of the Old Testament knows that the Law is at the core of its beliefs and disciplines. God gave His people the Law and expected them to obey it and observe to do all that was written in it. God also knew that this was not something they could do without a changed heart. The heart given to them at birth was not able to obey or respond to God. The Law exposed their weakness and sinfulness—their inability to do what He expected. That is why God had to give His people a new heart, a regenerated heart, a heart after His heart. People in the Old Testament responded to God the same way as those in the New Testament. God has never offered a relationship with His people based on works and behavior. It has always been about the heart. Ezekiel 11:19–21 probably explains this as best as any passage. Let me cite this passage in its entirety so that you can read it fully:

> "And I will give them one heart, and I will put a new spirit within you; and I will take the stony heart out of their flesh, and will give them an heart of flesh: that they may walk in my statutes, and keep mine ordinances, and do them; and they shall be my people, and I will be their God. But as for them whose heart walketh after the heart of their detestable things and their abominations, I will recompense their way upon their own heads," saith the Lord God.

Although this passage predicts a future time when Israel will be redeemed nationally, the points of the text are clear. Unless one has a heart changed by God, he will not be able to "walk in my statutes, and keep mine ordinances, and do them." Obedience to God and the Law was never something God expected of those who did not have a changed heart. Our Heavenly Father knew that His children needed a heart directed towards Him and He offered it to them. Without that, they would not be able to do the right things. In fact, God's people would often do the deeds of the Law in a mechanical way and God would rebuke them for that. Since a changed heart is so important to the Lord, it should be crucial to us, as well. Trying to have our children respond to us in a favorable way when their heart is far from us is the same picture of the Lord wooing His people to His favor when their heart was not with Him. Only a changed heart will satisfy.

The New Testament and the Heart

If what I have said is true for the Old Testament, then the same should be true for the New Testament. The major word for "heart," from which we get our English word, "cardiac," occurs 160 times. While that may not seem like much, try comparing this word with other words used in this portion of Scripture and you will find something rather interesting. The major word for grace occurs 156 times, love occurs 116 times, peace occurs 92 times, and mercy only 28 times. That alone should state how important God sees the heart. "Heart" can be found in 22 of the 27 New Testament books; the ones that don't contain it are the smallest books: Titus, Philemon, 2-3 John, and Jude. (Of these, only Titus has more than one chapter.) Even the word "grace" is missing in four books, and what theologian would not discuss the importance of grace to the New Testament? So, the fact that "heart" is missing in some of the smaller writings should by no means distract from its major importance in the New Testament. Let's take a closer look at some of the references:

1. Matthew 5:8 – "Blessed are the pure in *heart* . . ."
2. Matthew 5:28—Adultery measured by what is in the *heart*.
3. Matthew 6:21—"Where your treasure is, there will your *heart* be also."

4. Matthew 11:29—Christ talks about His *heart*.
5. Matthew 15:19—Evil proceeds from the *heart*. (The heart is the source of our sin; that is why we need a changed heart.)
6. Matthew 22:37—This is the classic response Jesus gives in response to the request about the greatest commandment—"Love God with all your *heart*" (and it's first on His list).
7. Luke 16:15—God knows the *heart*.
8. John 13:2—Satan takes over the *heart* of Judas.
9. Acts 5:3—Satan fills the *heart* of Ananias and Sapphira.
10. Acts 8:37—Philip explains evangelistically the importance of believing with your whole *heart*.
11. Acts 16:14—Lydia is converted as the Lord opened her *heart*.
12. Romans 10:9—Believe with your *heart*…
13. 2 Cor. 4:6—We are lost until God shines in our *hearts*.
14. Eph. 3:17—Christ is to dwell in our *hearts*.

Again, we are merely scratching the surface of the key Scriptures which discuss the vital nature of the heart.

When you examine the New Testament references, it is clearly the heart where our faith walk really begins. We start our physical life with a heart that is separated from God due to original sin passed down to us from Adam. Because he sinned, we are declared sinners (Romans 5:12). This means God does not live in our hearts as a place of residence and authority. The person from birth has an evil heart of unbelief (Hebrews 3:12). That is why Scripture mentions that we need to believe with our hearts (Romans 10:9–10). Our heart is the seat of all that we are. So much of our normal conversation reveals these same ideas. We talk today of a broken heart when someone is hurt. When someone is confused, they have a divided heart. When someone falls in love, they have given their heart away. A person who is harsh may be called heartless. When we scare someone, they say we have given them a "heart attack."

God's Word has made it clear that the heart is at the center of our lives, and so it is true in parenting. When the child's heart is not in line with God, you are simply putting a cover on a problem that will inevitably surface later. This is where many parents have misdiagnosed their child's problem. If a child rebels later in life and wants to have nothing to do with God, they often scratch their heads and wonder what happened. Why has my child gone astray? The problem is much deeper than that. I suspect that far too often the child has not gone astray, but merely begins to live out what has always been in their heart. If Judas can live three years with the disciples without them knowing he is on the wrong side, can't a child do the same right under Mom and Dad's nose? Of course they can! They become skilled at deception. Remember that their father (the devil), is a master deceiver. This is why it is so important to get the heart of your child at an early age. I cannot stress this enough. Remember, letting children decide about Sunday school, AWANA or other programs, Christian school, etc., is merely playing in Satan's hands. The early years should be years of immersion into the things of God. Failure to do so could have long-lasting spiritual effects that may never be recovered. For further study, I recommend you read Ken Hamm and Britt Beamer's book *Already Gone*. They masterfully detail the importance of getting the child early. Youth rarely leave the faith in college, because by then they are already gone. The real battleground is their heart, and if they fall in love with Jesus, that battle is won. The battle for the heart is the most critical battle of all.

5

Heart Attacks

In today's world, the words "heart attack" send a shivering wave of despair and fear into homes every day. These heart attacks often signal the demise of a family member, most typically (but not exclusively) as the person gets up in age. Heart attacks are the leading cause of death for men and women today; over 1.2 million occur every year.[1] I guess our hearts just were not made to last forever. What are the causes of the many heart attacks that happen every day, even to children? Well, there are a number of reasons, from genetics to poor habits to various health issues. Many times heart attacks can be prevented with proper diet, exercise, and overall self-care. But this is not a medical book, this is a spiritual book. So what about spiritual heart attacks? Spiritual heart attacks come from both the inside and the outside, and these attacks cannot be taken any more lightly than a physical heart attack. There are symptoms, signs, and warnings that abound, but unless you take this concern seriously, there is a good chance the heart damage will go undetected. The life you save here might be your child's life.

Inward Heart Attacks

In talking about the heart, Jesus corrected the idea of the "religious types" of his time. They were very concerned about ceremonial cleanliness, but not concerned about the heart. Jesus addresses the problem in Mark 7:18b-23:

---

1. Miniño AM, Murphy SL, Xu J, Kochanek KD. Deaths: Final data for 2008. *National Vital Statistics Reports*; vol 59 no 10. Hyattsville, MD: National Center for Health Statistics. 2011.

> "Do you not perceive that whatever enters a man from outside cannot defile him, because it does not enter his heart but his stomach, and is eliminated, thus purifying all foods?" And He said, "What comes out of a man, that defiles a man. For from within, out of the heart of men, proceed evil thoughts, adulteries, fornications, murders, thefts, covetousness, wickedness, deceit, lewdness, an evil eye, blasphemy, pride, foolishness. All these evil things come from within and defile a man." (NKJV)

Jesus warns that it is not that which goes into a man that is the problem, but what comes out. What comes out exposes the heart—it reveals that the real cause of concern has already taken root. In this section, we will focus first on the inward destruction of the heart.

Scripture says the heart is desperately wicked (Jer 17:9). I doubt if many out there would be willing to admit that! Why does Scripture say this about the heart? It explains that everyone is born with a wicked heart. That's not a very popular assertion, but it is certainly truthful. God makes it clear that man's heart is desperately wicked *from the day he is born*. If man is left to his own devices with no spiritual transformations, he will basically go down a path of evil. Why? That is the direction of the heart from birth. You don't have to teach a child to do wrong. It comes naturally to him and to her. You have to teach children to do good, or they will typically choose bad. Now that does not mean that everything they do will be evil, but the overall path is one away from God, which is evil.

The battle for the heart of every child is the most important battle that is waged for the child. We hear regularly that "a mind is terrible thing to waste." The strong emphasis to go after the minds of the children is great, but it doesn't get to the root of the problem. The area of interest ought to be the heart, and unless you understand that, the next generation will not turn to God. Our Lord always went after the hearts of those He encountered. As I mentioned earlier, He even said that the commandments were summed up by loving the Lord your God with all your heart. The heart is the key, not the mind. Give me a heart of a child, and I can teach it to think. Give me a mind of a child, and it will reason itself away from God. We are not losing a generation of kids because they don't know enough. More education is not the answer. The need is for transformation, and that is the battle for the heart. Statistics prove that the majority of people come to Christ at an early age. Get them early, or you may not get them at all. That is why it often takes a serious tragedy, or major issue, or health concerns to drive people to Jesus later in life. The mind has no answers for what the heart cannot embrace. This makes it clear that if we are going to really impact our children and make a difference in their lives, it will not happen with reasoning or discussions. The key is and will remain to be the heart. You can see this more clearly with a young lady who falls in love. The boy can be a loser from every direction, and yet the girl does not see it. Her friends and family all tell her that he is not the guy for her. She dismisses them all because her heart is doing all the discerning for her. And once her heart has been turned towards the guy, no amount of reasoning seems to suffice. Why? The heart is stronger than the mind.

So, the first priority to help prevent heart attacks is to get the heart in line with the Savior. That can only happen with a true saving experience. God made the heart too big for anything in this world to satisfy. Only he can change the heart. Without a saving, transforming encounter with Jesus, the heart is open to all kinds of external attacks. Pray daily for your child's heart and do everything humanly possible to lead them to Christ. If you want your child's heart, it all begins with them knowing Jesus and having Him sitting on the throne of his or her heart. The heart must be changed inwardly first before you'll ever be able to guard the outward.

Outward Heart Attacks

Some parents assume that once their child is a follower of Jesus, all the hard work is over. It's not! Satan knows that he cannot pluck us out of our Heavenly Father's hands, but he will do all he can to make us ineffective. He cannot get our heart, because it belongs to Jesus. But he can so attack the heart that it will become damaged and possibly cause someone to be put on the inactive list.

How many adults today basically just exist in body because of a physical heart attack? They live in a body but are predominantly restricted to a room, bed, or wheelchair. It is so sad to observe, especially knowing that that is not what any person would want. So the parents' primary concern should be to guard the children from those things or people that would want to attack the heart. And let me make it clear—very few children are able to be that discerning. Just as children will eat the wrong things that would hurt their physical heart (like McDonalds for all three meals every day and every week), so they don't have the discernment to make sure that they are on guard for that which will destroy their spiritual heart. Parents: this is your job. Do not take it lightly.

Not long ago I went to the doctor to get a general physical. He asked many questions about my heart. Although he did not ask specifically about my heart since I would not know how to answer those questions, he did ask relevant questions that gave him hints about my heart's health. He asked about my diet and exercise. He listened to my heart with a stethoscope. He checked my blood pressure and tested my cholesterol levels. Just about everything the doctor did had something to do with my heart. He was very concerned about my heart even though we were not relatives or friends; it was just his job. How much more should we as parents be concerned about our kids' hearts, which have been entrusted to us by our Heavenly Father? As much as we do all that we can to avoid a physical heart attack, we should try just as hard to avoid any spiritual heart attacks; both kinds are equally lethal! Let's look at some of the areas of concern.

Undue Stress on the Heart

Many things stress a child's heart, and they are often stressors brought on by parents. These are the kind of things that come from the outside which cause stress that the heart should never have to face. Much of this undue stress occurs is when parents allow things into the family that the child should never have to deal with at an early age. For example, the old idea of holding a marriage together for the sake of the children is fast fading. And I am sure that there are some couples who believe that their children are better off in a divorced home than living with the circumstances that they were in before the divorce. While I am not saying that there are not some situations in which this might actually be worth the discussion, for the most part, this is a lie from the enemy. Children who are the product of divorce, even years later in their own married lives, still share the pain of that hurt. Don't think for one moment that divorce does not stress the heart of your children, and it is stress that they ought not to have to suffer. They did not ask to come into this world, and they did not ask to go through a divorce.

Unwise decisions can also bring about a certain level of stress in the home. I don't believe children need to be a deciding part of the decision-making process, but carefully consider how your decisions will affect them. One such example is moving. Is there ever a time to move? (Of course, there are times when people don't have control over whether they move, especially when parents are with the military or in certain jobs. However, we are talking here about discretionary moves.) One of the things I hoped for and prayed was that I would not have to move my children from their friends and comfort zones. God was extremely kind to me and allowed that to happen, and I have pastored at the same church for 26 years. (Not all pastors have that luxury!) Children are often shuffled about from school to school, from church to church, from community to community, and the parents don't even consider the heart disease that can follow. Some children make great friends wherever, but still, the absence of that classmate from the fourth grade still seems to have an effect on them. Don't take it lightly. A decision of this nature should be bathed in prayer—make it on your knees!

Poor decision making can result in heart disease just as much as any poor physical choice. Just as many walk the streets today, not realizing that they are a breath away from a heart attack, so also are children suffering from diseases caused by their parents' ill-advised actions. The hearts of our children are to be guarded, and we are the ones given that responsibility.

Poor Eating Habits

Our generation has poor eating habits. Ask any nutritionist today and they will say again and again that we are killing ourselves by what we are eating and by what we are not eating. I will leave the physical part of this discussion up to the parents, but take great care to ensure that your children are eating correctly. Junk food, sodas, fast food, snacks, desserts, and other poor dietary decisions need to be monitored carefully to protect the physical hearts of your children. Children do not make wise decisions in this area, and parents need to be alert. Know what your kids are eating and what they are not eating.

But I want to also discuss the spiritual eating habits and diet of the children. Do you honestly believe that your children are capable of making wise spiritual decisions? Many children, when given the

Heart Attacks

opportunity to go to Sunday School, AWANA, youth events, or a Christian school will give a myriad of reasons why they should not go. For example, most kids would much rather sleep in or watch television or sports on a Sunday morning. Church will lose out if the kids are given the authority to make those kinds of decisions.

The same goes with the many different kinds of media access that these kids have today. If given the opportunity to watch a hot new show that all their friends are talking about (even if the show has questionable content), or watch a more edifying program, which do you think most children will do? Now I realize that many parents believe that their children would always pick the best, but let me ask you a question—do you always choose the best? The reason we have the privilege of I John 1:9 is because we are negligent and sometimes outright sinful. Our children are ourselves in miniature, and they are just as capable of sinful behavior as we are. That is why parents need to be on the alert. Satan is a roaring lion seeking whom he may devour (1 Peter 5:8), including our kids. Children need their parents to watch over them and protect them from the host of heart attack strategies that Satan will use.

Children left to fend for themselves choose snacks and other foods that, in moderation, will not harm them. But children do not have a built-in moderation barometer, so God gave to them parents. Children left to fend for themselves spiritually will make the same kinds of mistakes. Therefore, we need to be sure to help them have a proper diet, physical and spiritually.

What to eat: God's Word, spiritual events, wholesome books, family-approved movies (Many websites can give you the skinny on movies before you see them.), God-centered educational materials, magazines that honor God, and associations that will support your convictions as a family. Help them avoid diet-related spiritual heart attacks by filling their spirits with excellent, nourishing food.

What not to eat: Secular material that is unholy on any level. Too many parents allow just a little of the wrong into the family and wonder where their children get the ideas from. Never underestimate how a little stimulation or harmless entertainment in the wrong direction can send a child spiraling down a path of ungodliness. For example, do not assume everything Disney is acceptable and worthwhile. Our family has been to Disney and we love Disney, so I have no personal axe to grind here, but let me illustrate this point with one such popular Disney movie, *The Little Mermaid*. Please don't send hate mail after this, but think with me. Princess Ariel's father clearly tells her not to do something. She disobeys her dad, and in the end, everything turns out just fine. Some, of course, assume that their five-year-old daughter would never get that out of the movie. It is simply harmless entertainment and fun. But how many kids today think that they know more than their parents and rebel when their parents tell them to do something? Is it not possible that this seed was planted years ago in the innocence of a Disney movie? Is it worth the risk? Does that mean all Disney movies are evil and that our little cherubs are going to be robbed of a normal life? Not really, but parents need to be more informed about what their children are digesting. Be careful also with subtle things that may appear to be harmless, but can have lasting impact. Discuss those elements of the show with the child if you must watch it. Rewrite endings.

Some shows need to be off the radar entirely, such as shows that flaunt suggestive talk or lewd concepts. Shows that are anti-family need to be monitored, as well. Some years ago, I regularly watched the sitcom *Home Improvement*. It had so many funny components, and it appeared harmless. After all, it was a family that stayed together and learned together and provided entertainment. After a while, I noticed a few other things. Instead of Dad being wise and discerning as dads were in shows of years past, the dad in *Home Improvement* was often a bumbling idiot. Can you even imagine a show today with the title of *Father Knows Best*? Yet don't you want your children to believe that father really does know what's best for his kids? If they are continually bombarded by television and music with the idea that dads are dumb, what will they eventually believe about their own dad? It takes time to be discerning, but it is well worth the effort. And should you miss something in a particular show (as is quite likely), take that opportunity to teach the appropriate truths.

Lack of Exercise

Health clubs abound all over our country, along with all kinds of fitness gyms and home exercise DVDs and programs. They are great sellers around Christmas and early January, but many just collect dust as people fail to follow through on the commitment. How many adults have lifetime memberships to a gym/club, and hardly ever go there? Our hearts need to be physically fit if they are going to last a long life time.

Heart Attacks

As we look around at the youth of today, we see a generation of kids who are truly not in good physical condition. There might be many reasons for this, but one that certainly is on every list is a lack of proper exercise. As I mentioned earlier, schools talk about being healthy but don't have the funds or the inclination to help students put it into practice. Kids often come home after school and sit on the couch till bedtime. In the end, the children are eating junk food and playing video games on that comfortable sofa and are not getting enough exercise to develop the heart properly. As a result, the heart is ripe for disease and subsequent attack. Parents need to do a better job of getting their kids off the couch and into the exercise room. Again, don't leave this up to the children to decide, because they will, like anything else in nature, choose the path of least resistance.

Spiritual exercise is just as important as physical exercise, and it has eternal consequences. I mentioned in the previous section the importance of God's Word in the child's diet. Let me amplify that a little. Studying God's Word is a discipline that must be taught and encouraged. Our children need to know how to dig into Scripture and apply it to their everyday situations. When I entered Bible college at age 17, I really was biblically illiterate. Even though I grew up in a Christian home and attended church regularly, I did not have a good understanding of or handle on Scripture. I remember the first night in Bible college with my two new room-mates. One of them thought it would be a good idea to read the Bible together before we went to bed. I agreed, and they asked me to read from I John. I turned to John chapter 1. I never even knew there was a I John! I had it all around me, but it had not sunk into my heart. Encourage and help your children to study God's Word. Get them an age-appropriate Bible and even a Bible study book of some sort, such as devotions for teens, etc. Help them to memorize the books of the Bible. Help them to see how the situations in the Bible are similar to things they face in their own lives. They need to exercise their mind spiritually and often.

Other spiritually disciplines are helpful, as well. Encourage them to engage their friends, help others, and serve in the church. We took our children to the homeless shelter a few times to enable them to exercise spiritual gifts by serving meals and to learn about the needs of others. We did not want our children to make life all about themselves. We also tried to reach out to people who never had a family at Christmas. One such couple has become our adopted family members, and they are part of all our regular family celebrations. The more children exercise their hearts in these matters, the more they will find their hearts free from damage.

Concern about Family History

Another outward heart attack is generational heart disease that is passed to the children from the parents. Some diseased hearts are genetically caused. There is little a parent can do about the physical make-up of a heart, but we can do something about the family history and the spiritual heart.

Parents need to be cautious about generational sins—those which are passed down from family member to family member via the blood line. There certainly seems to be a pattern of concern that must not be overlooked. Why is it that families that are prone to alcoholism produce children who struggle with similar issues? There are many studies which examine these issues in much more detail, but the point is apparent: families can have certain problems which are passed on to the children. Certainly heart disease is one condition which has been proven to be hereditary. There might not be much you can do about the hereditary disease, but what about the avoidable spiritual diseases that harm the heart?

Parents need to see that God is the Great Healer. The sins of fathers do not have to pass on to the children. We need parents who will stand strong and break generational sins so that the children can be protected! It is one thing for heart disease to suddenly strike our children, but let's do all we can to shield them from what is clear. Just because Dad has the problem does not mean Johnnie needs to. If Dad is an idiot, is the kid doomed? God forbid!

Often Overlooked Areas That Attack the Heart

The Electronic World

The electronic world is a great danger to the child's heart today. The internet, just one such area, brings all kinds of pictures, stories, and information to your children in just a second or two. Parents need to be very careful about what children are viewing. And it is not just the computer; I heard of a parent who had trouble with the child's internet-accessible phone. Now this particular family was very careful, and the internet was password protected, plus they had certain blocks on the web. One day, however, this child walked down the street of their neighborhood and logged on to a neighbor's unprotected internet connection. The child found material that he had never had access to before. It can happen accidentally, and Satan will do all he can to make the material harm the child. Protection of these hearts must be a priority.

Games that they play can also be a hazard. Most games today have parental ratings, but who is measuring the ratings? Examine movies, media, and other electronics to be sure that they are espousing values you want your kids to have. Once the wrong things get into our children's minds, they are very hard to erase, and they will affect their heart for God. Only God can heal those heart conditions.

Because children often do not have the necessary discernment to make wise decisions, parents need to help guard their minds and decision-making process. But even with that guidance, there needs to be careful supervision. Again, you should have access to all their passwords and all their electronic devices. You should let them know that you will check periodically. I would also strongly warn against them having a computer or any internet-accessible device in their room at night. Kids need their sleep and their social networking may just interfere with both sleep and study. Keep an eye on their grades; if they are not doing well, it may mean that they are socializing too much. Additionally, keep in mind that there are predators out there who will not be merciful to your children. Many young children have fallen prey to people that they trusted over the internet. Also, do not let them have a television in their room. Is there really any sensible reason to have one there in the first place? Finally, know the music that is on their devices. I would suggest only allowing them to have Christian music. Maybe a secular artist is not necessarily evil, but once you open the door, it might be hard to get back to the correct path. Don't assume your child has the discernment necessary to detect bad lyrics. Some are obvious, but Satan is clever and he will use whatever to deceive. Just ask Adam and Eve.

I Heart Parenting

Sports

Participation in sports can help a child develop both mentally and physically. However, it is easy to over prioritize this area in your children's lives. It is an easy danger area to slip into. You start out very innocently and then become sucked into the world and pressure. There are many teams, many opportunities, and frequent practices. You don't want your child to be behind other athletes and you can do a lot of this as a family. So you miss a Sunday here or there. So you miss out on a few other church-related events. So they don't have time to connect with spiritual themes around the family, but sports is a good thing, right?

Yes, sports *can* be positive. But if Johnnie knows more about the latest football stats or his favorite players' achievements than about the Bible, you are in danger of having his god be the god of sports. You are producing a child that has an idol, and you are feeding that idol by catering to that. Where is God in all of this? And as the heart continues to draw towards sports, you are losing your child to the world. Is this what you desire?

Acceptance of Labels

Maybe you have never really considered this area before, but our society's acceptance of labels is a concern. Here are just a few: ADD, ADHD, hyperactive, terrible twos, rebellious teens, teenagers, strong-willed, etc. Now, let me be clear. There are some situations that require labels and there are cases where a child might need some form of medication due to certain chemical imbalances. I don't ever want a family to throw away medicines that have been prescribed by a caring and thoughtful doctor who truly understands their child. There are cases where medicine is the solution. However, I am not referring to those situations. What concerns me is that the labels children receive are used to justify their behavior. Take, for example, the phrase "terrible twos." My wife and I have lived through having two-year-old children and I can tell you that they are some challenging times. We even had the joy of having two at the age of two at the same time! Yes, there are some very real issues that begin to surface at age two. They become more independent as they can just about walk anywhere and reach anything. Their speech is improving rapidly, and they can carry on conversations well enough to call 9-1-1. They seem to have a lot of energy at that stage and unfortunately, the parents don't necessarily have as much stamina as they do! But does that mean that parents should let them get away with outrageous behavior? Does that make tantrums okay, since they are just "a phase"? The Bible doesn't seem to suggest that anywhere. In fact, it discourages that sort of behavior and talks about the value of self-control, thinking before we speak, etc. I realize that Scripture is not exclusively a parenting handbook, but it truly has much to say about parenting. What ought to be our guide? Should Scripture drive the parenting thought process or secular humanism?

Children are a gift from God and are made in the image of God. We need to see our children through the eyes of God and not secular thinking. Unless we maintain a clear, Biblical thought process, we will probably be parenting after the world.

Over my years as a pastor, I have rushed to the hospital to visit church members who have had heart attacks. In some cases, the heart attack came without warning. In other cases, the heart attack could have been avoided. How sad to know we could have done something to have prevented that attack!

Parents, your children's hearts are under attack. You need to do all you can with God's help to shield them from the attacks of this world. What a shame for them to face a heart attack that you could have prevented! Guard your child's heart with all diligence. They are worth it!

6

What Kind of Parent Are You?

THERE ARE MANY DIFFERENT styles of parenting, and every couple has particular (and sometimes unique) ways to respond to situations. Some of this has to do with how you were raised as a child, some with what you have observed, and some with influences that have shaped you. Read over these styles carefully and see if you can locate the one that most defines you. We will end the section with the Biblically-based parent who goes after the heart of his/her child; that's the one we should all strive to be.

My Kids Never Do Anything Wrong Parent

Some parents simply will never acknowledge that their child is capable of wrongdoing. Today, if a child gets in trouble at school, it is the school's fault. If a child is not getting enough playing time, it is the coach's fault. If a child "makes errors in judgment," it is because they hang around that other kid. Parents today are raising a generation of kids who do no wrong, and God forbid if you ever try to tell them something about their kid. You can be sure you will be left off the next Christmas card list.

Parents need to wake up. These precious little darlings are capable of every sin in the book, just like their "perfect" parents. To continue to come to the rescue of your little cherubs is only going to make a monster out of them. You are not going to rescue them at their job, college, or marriage. They need to accept that life is not always fair, and sometimes the reason that they are in the mess that they are in is because they sinned and did wrong.

Maybe you can relate to this scenario. When my girls started playing soccer, I discovered a symptom of current psychology. All children, no matter how badly they played, even if they sat on the sidelines all

What Kind of Parent Are You?

year, received a trophy. The team that lost all year received the same trophies as the team that won. While this is well-intentioned to build up self-esteem, it doesn't reflect life very well. The boss isn't going to give you a raise for just holding down a chair during the year! The danger of this type of thought is that the kids grow up believing that life owes them rewards. They should pass the class even if they didn't do the work. They should get on the honor roll if they achieve average grades.

With society promoting the idea that children's self-esteem is all important, it's easy to lose sight of the idea that our children are sinners. Kids feel like they should be rewarded all the time—the problem is *too much* self-esteem! Yet we buy into the idea and begin promoting the mindset when they are still very young. Every problem they cause is someone else's fault, and they feel few consequences. They broke the vase because someone put it too close to the edge of the table. He uses bad words regularly because they hear the kids at school do it. If she is driving too fast, it's because the speed limit sign was covered by weeds. If my child was given a detention, then surely it was someone else's fault.

Parents need to wake up to the reality that children sin and are capable of doing all kinds of sins. If you continue to excuse their behavior instead of facing it straight on, you are going to develop a heart that is not pliable to God. Repentance for sinful acts is a healthy thing that should be learned at an early age. Don't rob them of this great blessing by giving them a way to feel as if they hadn't sinned in the first place. And if they are ever wrongfully accused, take heart; their Savior modeled it well for them. What a teaching opportunity is lost when you become more concerned about defending your child than teaching them the joy of sorrow for sin and repentance!

If there comes a time when it is very clear that your child was wronged, there are some proper steps to take to defend him. But go to those in authority with a humble and meek spirit without any accusations or condemnation. You may not have all the information. Go to seek answers, and not to promote preconceived ideas. Don't just take your child's word for it. But don't go for every little infraction in life or you will be a hindrance in your child's heart. Your children need to know that things happen for a purpose and leave the results in God's hands. They need to learn it as a child so that as an adult, they don't run from church to church because their feelings are hurt. Raise up children who can deal with their sin in a godly fashion like a King David, who admitted his sin, repented, and modeled for us a man after God's own heart.

Head in the Sand Parent

Very similar to the previous example is the type of parent who has their head in the sand. They choose to simply trust whatever their children say and never examine it closely. I have heard parents say, "I respect my child's right to privacy and would never check up on them." Go ahead and let me know what the sand looks likes from below the surface.

Parents who believe in absolute privacy for their children give their children an opportunity to delve into inappropriate things, and many will. You need to have all their passwords for all electronics. You need to know what they are watching. You need to be fully aware of where they are going, the event they want to attend, the house that has the party, the one who may be driving the car. Be the guardian of their hearts, because once they have been scarred, it will make your work much more difficult.

I know that most kids ask their parents, "Don't you trust me?" You need to answer: "That is not the issue. I know Satan and I know he will try to deceive you." That is one of the reasons we have the Holy Spirit and the Scriptures and friends, and that is why God gave parents to children. God does not just leave us to do whatever. He gives us that which will help us stay on the narrow road. Parents—if you choose to keep your head in the sand, your child might just become a statistic, and you will have given them the license to do so.

How many parents out there today would love to go back and change the permission that they gave their child on that fateful night? How many wish that they had never given in to allow their daughter to go with that guy? How many wish they had never let their child go to that party? How many wish that they had screened their friends better, chosen a different school, watched their clothes better? Those parents who have been honest with me over the years have often said, "I wish I had been more alert to what they were doing. I was so busy at work, play, or church, that I didn't pay attention to my child's whereabouts and activities." If you don't begin early, you may lose out in the end.

My parents "trusted" me as a young teenager because I had never given them reason not to trust me. But, this was not an indiscriminate trust and freedom to do whatever. They examined who my friends were and saw how I behaved with them and protected my heart from many things. I was not allowed to date certain girls, go to certain places, attend certain parties, etc. At the time, I did not appreciate their efforts. Today I have a lovely wife, four beautiful children, and a blessed ministry. Had my parents not protected my heart during those vulnerable years, I might not have any of that today. Parents need to get their heads out of the sand and be more alert. The Bible compares the devil to a hungry lion, and your children are on his menu—while you're busily examining grains of sand!

I Turned Out Okay Parent

How many parents want to take their current position in Christ and assume that their children will follow the same path? They assume that since they turned out all right, even with this and that problem in their lives, their children will do the same thing. News flash: You may be the exception to the rule. Yet parents may permit their child to do things by using the following excuses:

1. I went to public school and I'm not a maniac today.
2. I did not attend Sunday school or youth groups but I go to church regularly now.
3. I came to Christ later in life, so my kids will be able to do the same.
4. I turned my life around after I got married.
5. I sowed my wild oats early as all kids do and got right later in life.
6. I did drugs and alcohol and now I have given them all up.
7. I listened to rock music when I was younger, and it was fine.
8. I watched some bad movies and they don't bother me.
9. I viewed some pornographic material as all boys do and I am ok.
10. I experimented with a lot of things in school/college and they made me better/wiser.

Some may not want to go quite that far, but it is implied by the way that they allow their children to spread their wings in life. This battle often surfaces in the home between the parents. Typically one parent is more lenient than the other. One parent advocates freedom: "Don't be so hard on them. All their friends are doing it. We don't want our kid to be a social outcast. They need to fit in." The other parent lobbies for limits, discipline, or wise choices. And so the battle of parents on permissions begins to cause much stress in the home. I believe that if one parent wants to put the brakes on something, it should cause the other to put the brakes on. God may be sparing you from some pain!

This also works in the area of clothing. I have often visited the mall and wondered what dad allowed their child to leave the house dressed like that. Some moms may actually be living out their teen years by giving their child permission to dress provocatively. The mom may have been a head turner, and she is simply reliving her wild youth years. Be very careful. Times are different, and just because you dressed provocatively and "survived" unscathed, your daughter may not. Additionally, think how many boys struggled with lust because you turned them on with your attire. Maybe they would have lusted anyway, but do you want to contribute to their sin?

Parents need to stop parenting through repetition of their parents' mistakes. Yes, you may have turned out fine, and it may be God's grace that you turned out that way. Now He leaves it up to you to change it. He has given you the knowledge and the grace to break that mold. You have been called by God to raise a generation of God-fearing children that will rise above the level that you have achieved. Your goal is to raise them to have a heart after God, not to give them a smorgasbord of what the world has to offer.

The Oft-Repeating Parent

I am sure by now that you have already guessed that I have a slightly sarcastic nature. Ok, more than slightly. In this section I may have to take the silencer off. After raising four children and being in many situations with other parents, I have to tell you that it is fun to watch parents raise their children. My favorite parent is probably the oft-repeating parent. This is how they parent:

1. I am going to count to ten and you had better…
2. Won't you please, please, please, pretty please do this for Mommy?

3. How many times do I have to keep telling you the same thing over and over again?
4. One more time and Daddy is going to…
5. This is now the fifth time that I have called you!

It reminds me of a humorous story that I heard about a little boy who was playing in his back yard with a neighbor kid. They were busy in the sand box and the little boy's mom called him, but he kept right on playing. A few minutes later and she called again. The neighbor boy, thinking that maybe his friend had not heard, told him that his mom was calling him. The boy said, "Yes I know, but she only means it on the third call. I don't have to come till then." What this kind of parenting teaches is delayed obedience. And delayed obedience is actually disobedience. What if little Johnnie is out in the road or near a venomous snake and you call out to him, but he is trained to hear the third call and ignore the rest? Children need to be taught that immediate obedience is expected of them and will be enforced.

Does God expect immediate obedience or does He count to three for us? Can you imagine Jesus calling Peter to follow Him and Peter, sitting in his boat, saying, "I am on the fish big time and can't stop right now. Let me take a rain check on that!" Do you think that would have been acceptable to the Savior? The oft-repeating parent is a lazy parent who does not want to face the necessary actions that are required to bring a child to the next level. But by doing so you are creating a heart of rebellion that will surface later in the child's walk with Jesus. In those early years, parents need to soften the child's heart to hear the voice of God clearly and often. How sad when parents help their children turn a deaf ear to God's call for their lives.

The Caving-in Parent

This is the parent that would rather give in than deal with the struggle of standing on what they believe is best. Of course, it makes life easier to just give in, and kids are a whole lot more enjoyable to be around when you give them what they want. I am sure that many parents have struggled with this and have given in to something because they just were not up for the fight. Parenting is hard work.

The problem is, if young children are brought up under this kind of parenting, it is only going to lead into that which is more difficult later. For a small child, we can wonder, what harm is one more slice of cake? Besides, they will stop whining, and I will be the good dad. "Dad is the fun parent" they'll sing, "He gives me chocolate cake!" Yes, Dad may be great for the moment, but you are setting up a precedent, and precedents like that have a way of instantly becoming the expected norm, even if they were at first given in unusual circumstances.

Children who throw temper fits in public can be an embarrassment to you. Spanking in public can bring social services to your house, but ignoring poor public behavior may bring the police to your house later in life. What is a parent to do? If at all possible, take the child immediately to the car and head home. You can explain in the privacy of the car that they have a special treat waiting for them at home, especially since they have just ruined your day. If you cannot leave, maybe a private area can be found to take care of business. If neither of those is possible, you may have to speak firmly to them and remind them that you are going to take care of this when you get home. Warning: don't forget to do so. But avoid caving in to the demands of your children whenever possible. Once you do so, it will be etched in your child's mind and they will come back to it later when it most benefits them.

I heard of a story where a little boy (about 5 or so) used to hold his single mom hostage to this strategy. If they were ever out and he wanted something he would rant and rave and let her know that if she did not comply, he was going to take off all his clothes. This mortified the mom, and it worked well for the child. He got everything he ever asked for. One time, he tried the same thing on the dentist: "I am not getting up in that chair and if you try to make me, I am going to take off all my clothes."

The dentist had had one of those days and he was not willing to deal with this kid. "Do what you have to do, but you're getting up in this chair," he said.

The boy started disrobing and the dentist allowed him to do so. Once all his clothes were off, the dentist picked him and put him in the chair and worked on his teeth. After he was finished, the dentist picked up the clothes and threw them to the mom in the waiting room as the buck naked boy exited. (Obviously this was years ago because today the dentist would be arrested!) The hygienists could not believe what had happened and warned him he would probably hear back from that mom. Sure enough, that evening the mom called, and the dentist waited to hear the screams. But there were no reprimands. Instead she thanked the dentist and explained how her child had her hostage to this for over a year. She did not know what to do. She thanked her dentist over and over for his assistance.

Now by no means am I recommending that action today because of all the legal issues that would follow. But my point is this: caving in to children's demands at an early age will only set up greater issues later. Children need to know who is in charge. They need to know that early. If not, expect a struggle for years to come. God does not cave in to our whining. He is a God who has standards that must be met and kept at all times. He will not be held hostage by our demands, and neither should parents.

The Absentee Parent

The absentee parent is the parent who is a parent only because his/her name might be on the birth certificate. Parents need to remember that children did not ask to come into this world. There is not a storehouse of children up in Heaven asking to be taken to our homes. Two people come together and with the help of the work of God, a baby is born. And with that baby comes great responsibility. There is no room for AWOL parents.

Allow me to challenge all of you who are absentee parents out there: if you took the time to "make" the baby, then you must take the time to be the parent of the baby. No exceptions allowed. And if you helped "make" the baby when you were not married to the girl, then man up and accept responsibility. In olden days there were shotgun weddings. If a boy got a girl pregnant, the father of the girl would come looking for the boy with a shotgun, and the wedding would take place that day. I realize that there might be some extenuating circumstances, but there are too many absentee parents, especially dads. (Some moms, of course, are equally as absent, but it appears to be predominately dads.)

Dads who are workaholics, pleasure seekers, television addicts, etc., are too often absent from parenting and consumed with self-gratification. Take, for example, the idea of workaholics. They say they are building their career, or working to provide for their family. They're doing all this work for the kids, and the kids should appreciate it, they say. What the child needs is his or her dad, not stuff. Most kids would readily trade the best "stuff" for more time with Dad! The statistics suggest the average parent spends only a few minutes each day with his or her children, while history records that Suzanna Wesley (mother of John and Charles who were great servants of the Lord) spent an hour a day with her children, and she had 13! Do the math. Be engaged with your children. Take an interest in their interests. Watch them grow and determine their strengths and weaknesses, encouraging the former and working to overcome the latter. Too much of that is left to others such as teachers and friends. The heart of your child has been entrusted to you, parents, and you cannot abdicate that privilege to anyone else.

The Biblically-Balanced Parent

All of the above models have been the kind of examples you do not want to be. This last example is the one we should all aim at being. There are many facets to the biblically-balanced parent, but here is an overall definition: this parent is the man or woman who seeks God with all their heart and does all that they are led to do by God to lead their child to be a child after the heart of God. How that is going to be fleshed out in the lives of the family might look a little different in each home. But at the end of the day, you need to be loving God with all your heart and helping your child down the same path. If this indeed is your goal and you do all you can to reach that goal, you will be a parent after God's own heart. That is the thrust of this book. May we as parents accept the challenge to be the Biblically-balanced parent who goes after the hearts of their children for the Lord.

But what does a Biblically-balanced parent look like? I am sure if I asked people from diverse places and circumstance, they would offer all kinds of differing thoughts on the exact make-up of a Biblically-balanced parent. Yet, I also believe that there are a few truths that cannot be overlooked. This is the kind of parent every one of us ought to seek to be.

Of course, he must not be like the previous examples listed in the chapter. Learn that these parents are not Biblically-balanced and take great care to avoid these kinds of behaviors. Take the time to truly examine those illustrations in the first part of this chapter and correct any actions that resemble those lifestyles.

Second, we don't have to figure this out on our own. We have the perfect Heavenly Parent and He is described in great detail all throughout Scripture. Our Heavenly Father is the Example that we need to emulate in all our actions as a parent. If we learn from His example, then we have truly learned from the greatest Father ever. One word of caution: that is a high example to follow. Needless to say, we are going to fall short of the goal of perfection He has given to us. But that should not stop us from learning from His example and giving it our best effort. Matthew 5:48 says it well: "Be ye therefore perfect even as your Father, who is in Heaven is perfect."

So, what characteristics of God our Father should we incorporate into our parenting?

1. Our Heavenly Father is loving.
2. Our Heavenly Father is patient.
3. Our Heavenly Father is fair.
4. Our Heavenly Father is kind.
5. Our Heavenly Father is consistent.
6. Our Heavenly Father is always ready.
7. Our Heavenly Father is firm.
8. Our Heavenly Father is discerning.
9. Our Heavenly Father is holy.
10. Our Heavenly Father is gentle.

I doubt that this list has exhausted the Scriptural picture of our Heavenly Father, but it should have at least given us a picture to begin our quest for emulating Him. Remember that He loves those children more than we could ever do, so expect Him to help you become what He has called you to be. Be the Biblically-balanced parent that your children can admire, resemble, and emulate when they are parents.

Part Two

The H-E-A-R-T of Parenting

Over the next several chapters, I want to offer some suggestions on how to get to the heart of your child. Each chapter will address a different letter of the word "Heart." Then, after we have examined each letter, I want to close this section with some practical application to go from information to transformation, a truly changed heart.

7

The "H" Challenge of the Heart—Heart

Before the Child Arrives

IT ALL BEGINS WITH the heart. I realize that I have stressed that already, but I am not sure it can be stressed enough. But how does a parent get to a child's heart and keep the heart so that the child is capable of being all God wants her/him to be?

Believe it or not, the path can begin before the baby is even born. Of course, most of you reading this book already have children. Nevertheless, I believe it is important to stress the importance of early going after the heart, even before the child is born. It begins with early, constant, and consistent saturation of the truths of God. To get a proper start on parenting, it must begin with the parents and their walk with God. So often, couples with young children say, "We need to find a church so we can raise our children properly." I appreciate the step in the right direction, but that direction ought to have been mapped out years earlier. If the thought is only just now occurring to you as you contemplate having children, let's explore how a parent begins this process.

Before the child is ever conceived, it is important for the "expecting" couple to put some care and thought into their own journey. I am not sure anyone is ever ready for child. Some have even said that they are going to wait to have children until they can afford it. Good luck with that thinking! Is anyone ever ready? Every couple should begin to talk about their own walk with Christ and ask themselves if this is a home in which a baby could flourish and be nurtured. Don't wait until the baby has arrived to debate these issues. Begin before the wedding day in the pre-marital counseling class to talk about the Christian home that they are beginning to develop. Having a child is not simply a sexual act. It is much more than that. It is a God-given responsibility and privilege that one is not to take lightly. How prepared are you for this entrance of life? Far too often the only discussion surrounds the finances. Can we afford a child? The answer to that is a resounding "NO" for many, but finances are not the issues at hand. Can you "afford" to bring a child that is a gift from God into a home where the parents are not surrendered to God? That is a much more important question. How does a couple get themselves ready to become parents?

Although we are a body, each individual member must walk the walk and give themselves totally to Christ to be all God wants them to be. That kind of home ought to be a home where love is the center and Christ is at the head. There ought to be regular quiet times/devotions, prayer, service, and church membership in a Bible-believing church. A baby ought to grow up in a home that is solidly Christian, not one that is trying to learn how to be a Christian. Now please don't panic if you have not put these things in place before children. I am just trying to give the best case scenario. One can play catch up, but it is always better to have these disciplines in place first before the grand arrival.

Another important area involves the parenting style in the home. It is more than likely that husband and wife have grown up in different homes with different kinds of standards. What are your views on birthing, education, discipline, baby sitters, bedtimes, etc.? Once the child arrives, the couple will be too busy to even have time to discuss these concerns, and before you know it, the child is going to college. Believe me, after seeing my children grow up before my eyes, I can say with confidence that time really does fly! I remember hearing adults tell me to treasure each moment with my child, because it will go fast! Yet as I changed the diaper for the third time in five minutes at 3 AM, I would often say, "Yeah, right!" Now, how I would love to have all my kids back home! I am not going to be a happy empty nester. Parenting has been a blessed journey for me and I would do it all over again in a heartbeat. Kids are simply awesome. Don't waste a minute.

Now after the many discussions have been worked through, the couple believes that they are now ready to be parents. Again, is anyone really ready to be a parent? Never, but at least you have begun to discuss the important issues and hopefully have come to many resolutions on where you ought to be in the parenting realm. If not, slick commercials will have you buying everything under the sun to meet the needs of this new generation, and who would want their kid behind when they start kindergarten? Give them the newest and hottest and your kid will be the brightest. (If you are buying into that already, I have some excellent real estate that I would like to sell you in the Atlantic Ocean.) Work through these issues early and as completely as possible.

After the Child Arrives

Skip ahead to the day you bring the baby home. What a delight. As you are driving home from the hospital with Mom and baby in the back seat, and of course baby in a child protective car seat, many questions will flood your mind. What is next? Are we prepared? What do we do? And one of the saddest things about all this is that the hospital does not even send you home with a manual.

The baby is finally home and the first issues are fairly simple: sleep and feeding and changing. Even so young, babies will work their way into your heart, so you typically give a lot of thought to these early questions. How much sleep is normal? Should they sleep on their side, back, or belly? Crib or bassinette? Do they sleep in their own room or their parents'? This all leads me to a story about our first encounter with our baby at home. I am such a guardian of my sleep. I do not like to stay up late and do not like to be interrupted when asleep. I arise early and so need my sleep. My wife and I had our discussion about our baby and I made it clear that the baby will sleep in her own room. We have a bassinette that has been handed down through our family. It was positioned by my wife's side and she laid our girl in it for the night and went to the bathroom to get ready for bed. I decided that for a few moments it might be nice to have the baby at my side. I moved the bassinette to my side, and placed my arm on her and patted her to sleep. When my wife came out of the bathroom, we were both asleep, and my hand was still on our baby. Needless to say, she stayed in our room for weeks. Sweet stories aside, though (and don't we all have them?) we need to focus at all times on how that adorable baby can grow up to be a man or woman of God.

I would suggest early on taking control of the home. If you let the child dictate when they sleep, when they eat, and when they are held, you are setting the groundwork for child-centered parenting. These early years are important. Feed your child properly and let them sleep a healthy amount and hold them often. But please make sure you are setting the stage for who is in control. Early habits begin to form the pattern of behavior. Feeding on demand to stop a baby from crying when she is not hungry allows them to begin to be in control. Again, never neglect proper feeding of your child, but be cautious of the standard that is set early on. You will quickly learn the difference between a cry for a need and a cry for a want. (By the way, doctors continue to state that some level of crying is healthy for the development of a child.) You will not get their hearts if they are in the lead.

After these early precedents are clearly established, the walking and talking years begin. These are some amazing years! They have already begun to show their personality, their laugh, their joy, and now their mannerisms begin to appear. The child's strong will surfaces. Giving in to a strong-willed child is extremely serious. Strong-willed children have the ability to run and ruin a home. They can be so demanding on parents that if you begin to give in to them while they are young, you are forming a heart that is set on self-satisfaction. Many strong-willed children can be taught early on through feeding on schedules and sleeping on schedules, but some will even get through that stage with a strong will. Their will must be broken early, but not their spirit. The heart from birth has a desire to be its own boss; some just call it total depravity. A child with a strong will that is not challenged and redirected towards God is heading for many years of resistance to authority. Parents have a choice early on—either direct the heart of their child to be under their guidance or accept the consequences that inevitably follow. This parenting model can be seen in the call of Jesus to His disciples. He asked them to leave their nets and their boats and carry a cross and follow Him. The reason for this was a challenge to the control of the heart. Who is going to be in charge? Early on, your children need to know who is in control.

As soon as your child is able to understand the Gospel, explain it clearly. Make sure that they understand and are able to grasp the truths. This must be the first and foremost endeavor of the parents: leading their child to Christ. Since Scripture promises that He will never leave your child, what a blessing to know your child is always in the care of Jesus.

The "H" Challenge of the Heart—Heart

Practical Suggestions for Going After the Heart

There are many practical ways for parents to go after the heart. I would strongly recommend a good, Bible-believing church that has various venues for teaching the children. Put your children in a setting where their listening ear is directed towards God. Some churches have church for kids when the adults are in worship. I believe ministries like this are a good suggestion. There are, of course, families who prefer their children to worship with them, although I do believe that children learn better with age-sensitive teaching. Additionally, there are times children should not hear the adult themes in worship such as family issues, abortion, homosexuality, etc. Regardless, at least the Word is getting in, and that is a good thing. Also, emphasize Sunday school, some sort of scriptural training such as AWANA, and other types of children's educational methods. Find a church for you and your family that will assist you in shaping the child's heart in the early years, especially as you go after their heart.

Another wise suggestion is to have family devotions and reading of good Christian books at bedtime. There are also many great video tools for children that are age sensitive and greatly inspiring. Most children love the sing-along videos and others that portray Biblical stories in a child's world. Later, as your children can be taught the more mature version of the stories, they already have the foundation laid for Biblical advancement. The heart needs to be turned towards God early and often, and then to have it cultivated with strong Biblical themes. Secular shows may have excellent educational advantages, but the greater foundation is spiritual development in these early years. I call it spiritual saturation. Too many families incorporate secular saturation (sports, television, music, etc.), and wonder why their child has little spiritual desire. Saturation with spiritual things can develop an appetite for God that will last forever.

Make prayer over your children a priority. Pray every day for your children with specific prayers: future mates; discipleship; growth; and most important, a heart after God. Pray for them by their bed and then throughout the day. The world is not friendly to the family and every day you are fighting a battle. These battles must be won by prayer. Again, the idea is saturation. Learn every way you can possible go after your child's heart for spiritual transformation. Listen to what others have done. Read diligently the writings of those who have raised godly children. Don't do everything another family has done, however, since each family is unique, but learn all you can to bring every child to Jesus, and then saturate their heart with the Savior. I believe you will see the heart respond to its Maker, when it is properly directed from an early age.

I have basically described a two-pronged effort to go after the heart. First, there is the effort called salvation—bring every child to a saving knowledge of Jesus. Second, there is saturation—bring every child to a daily growth in Jesus. Together, these two efforts will raise the chances for your child to have a heart after God, and a heart that is honoring to you.

The heart is not going to comply easily. It has been under the influence of the evil one since birth. There will be a struggle, since you "wrestle not with flesh and blood, but against principalities, against powers," and spiritual wickedness (Eph 6:12). Here is where the line is drawn in the sand. Here is where we face our Alamo or Waterloo or Normandy. Win this battle and you instantly have the power of the Holy Spirit living inside your child. That does not mean there won't be battles, but victory is more reasonable with a child whose heart is turned towards God.

8

The "E" Challenge of the Heart—Entrance

THE NEXT LETTER IN the word *heart* is E, which I have labeled the entrance to the heart. We know that the heart at birth is away from God. (I am not discussing what happens when a child dies before he or she is able to respond in faith to Christ. If you are interested, I would strongly recommend Dr. John MacArthur's excellent work on this subject, *Safe in the Arms of God*. He valiantly defends the heavenly destination of babies if they die before they are able to embrace faith.) Scripture is clear that the heart of a child must be changed to be in a right relationship with God. This cannot happen through baptism, parents, church membership, or any other deed. The heart of a child can only be changed by a process Scripture calls being born again (see Chapter Two).

What I want to emphasize here is the importance of guarding the heart both before and after the conversion experience. Salvation is not the end of the battle. It is the most important component of the battle, but being born again does not make one perfect. Parents are not perfect, and neither are kids. I love the bumper sticker that reads, "Christians are not perfect, just forgiven." That holds true for parents and children. Possessing a redeemed heart does not mean that a child is not going to slip and fall. That is where the sweet truth of confession and repentance plays a great role.

In the process of the entire salvation experience (that which leads to the decision and that which follows after), parents need to be guardians of their child's heart. The heart of a child is so weak and fragile. Have you not seen a child broken-hearted over a missing crayon? You can see a crushed heart of a child when their sock falls off, or when they cannot find their blanket at night. I remember going to the stores at midnight, hoping one was open so I could buy a pacifier that my daughter had to sleep with every night. She was broken-hearted that we could not find it at home, so out goes Dad in the middle of the night. Why? Because my child's heart was broken and I needed to do all I could do to mend her heart and guard it from any further pain. It is part of being a parent. We are guardians of their hearts, especially when they are too young to guard their hearts themselves. Proverbs 4:23 says (NIV), "Above all else, guard your heart, for it is the wellspring of life." The KJV says it this way: "Keep your heart with all diligence for out of it are the issues of life." The idea of keep means to keep watch or guard. Since children are unable to do so, it is the role of the parent.

This is one of the many reasons I support Christian education. Just ask yourself some questions: who would you permit to babysit your child? Who would you list as guardians should something happen to you as parents? (By the way, every parent ought to have a will. You don't want the state or your family fighting over the guardianship of your children.)

I believe this guardianship also includes friendships. Do you honestly believe your child is able to discern the best kids to have friendships? Who usually gets picked on the playground? The coolest kids are the ones everyone wants to join with and hang out with, but that does not mean that they are the best kids to associate with. Bad company also corrupts good morals (I Cor. 15:33). Now I can hear someone saying, "This takes a lot of work, and who really has the time to do these kinds of things?" The issue is not who has the time, but what do you value as the worth of your child? We are willing to invest the time in taking them all over to play sports or attend amusement parks, and we are willing to spend much money to make sure that they have the best of everything, but the greatest gift you can give is to guard them with all diligence. I don't believe any cost is too great in guarding our children.

Many parents lock their windows of their house and lock their doors at night. Why do they do this? They do this to prevent intruders from coming in and tearing up the house and possibly hurting someone in the house, especially a child. The laws require small children and infants to be in child protective seats. I remember when our first was born; it was made clear to us that in order to take Mom and baby home from the hospital, we must have an approved, child-safety car seat. The hospital saw their need to guard our child. I also remember the pediatrician later asking if we had any guns in our house. Personally, it is none of his business, but he was concerned about guarding our children. The doctors also suggest certain shots to guard our children from certain diseases. Our dentist even had a special application that they applied to our children's teeth to prevent decay and to guard their mouths. Later in life they wore a mouth guard to play sports. All this is certainly good and has its place.

But the guardians of a home are the parents, and particularly the dad. We must find the entrances to our kids' hearts (their house) and guard them. Whatever it takes, I would imagine any true-blooded dad would go to any extreme to protect his family. We had a situation in our family when our youngest was a baby where someone tried to harm our family. At that time, we were living next to the church in a church-owned house called a parsonage. We had a small car with a "Baby on Board" sign on the back window. Someone had given that to us and I thought it was cool. On this particular day, I was at home having lunch with my beautiful wife and charming little daughter. We heard a knock at the door, and my wife answered it. I was sitting at the lunch table and our daughter was in view of the door in a playpen. The man stumbled a little and asked for directions. My wife gave him the information and closed the door—all the while the visitor did not see me or know anyone else was home. In less than a minute, he was back. This time, my wife wisely asked me to go to the door. When I opened the door, the man was greatly startled. You could tell he was not expecting me. He stuttered and stammered and requested the time and then left. I became concerned, looked out the window, and noticed his car was an out-of-state vehicle; the door was left open and the car was idling. I took down the tag number and called the police. Why? I am the guardian of my family.

The following Sunday, while reading the paper, I noticed that a man had kidnapped a woman and a baby and had taken them across state lines, in addition to a number of other criminal acts. As I began to study the article more closely, I realized that it was the same man who had been at our house just minutes before he took another woman a few miles from us. Had I not been the guardian of our family, who knows how our story would have ended. You would think guarding your home would be obvious, yet week after week parents are letting intruders into their homes who take their children captive, and they are not even aware of the ongoing damage!

I Heart Parenting

Jesus Christ calls Himself the Door (John 10:9), which means that He is the entranceway to Eternal Life. He later confirms that by saying that He is "the Way, the Truth, and the Life; no man comes to the Father, but by me" (John 14:6). We all can understand the picture of a door. Most of us live in houses or apartments and they all have one major entrance door. In the Old Testament, there were many cities that had walls. These walls all had an entrance way that was called the gate. Elders and leaders, and of course guards, were often at the gates. Business was sometimes transacted at the gates. The gates were central to the life of any city. And any city that intended to have a future had better guard the gates. A failure to guard your doors and entrances to your home leaves it open to the real possibility that your house will be violated. That is why many homes have locks on their doors. No one is allowed in the house without the owner's permission.

Now imagine that there is a knock on your door, and you look out the window and notice that it is someone on America's Ten Most Wanted list. Would you open the door and let that person in? Would you welcome them into your home? Would you give them full access to your home and all your family? Here are my children, my wife, my dog—enjoy? No sensible, God-fearing man would ever allow someone to enter his house if they knew in advance that this person was dangerous and planning to do some harm. Why? Because we are the guardians of our doors, and we are not going to let anyone come into our lives (homes) and hurt our families. We will even fight to the end for their protection. We see that as our call and duty.

Now let us probe that thought a little deeper. Are you being as alert as possible about the entrance to your home? In particular, are you being as alert as possible about the entrance to your child's heart? We will do all we can to guard our physical doors, but are we being as careful with their hearts, the spiritual door to their lives? Proverbs 4:34 says in the KJV that we are to guard the heart, with the imagery of standing guard as a sentry. Can you imagine trying to get past the guards at the White House, or some other very important place in the world? No one would leave a place of importance open to any person who cared to just drift into the building. I remember visiting Vladimir Lenin's tomb years ago and seeing his embalmed body in a clear, closed up casket. You could not get anywhere near him since it was heavily guarded, and I respected that. If I had tried to get closer I would not be here writing

The "E" Challenge of the Heart—Entrance

this book today! Unfortunately, we are not going to get the same respect from a fallen world that would love to ensnare our children and make them like the children of the world; they go after our children's hearts. Just as much as we parents desire to guard the heart, the world desires to capture the heart. The whole world lies in the hands of the wicked one and he knows the importance of drawing the heart away for his purposes. Let the battle of the heart begin. Guard the hearts of your children just as you would the door of your house, with all diligence. Put locks on the heart and admit only those who will benefit and not harm your family. But the problem often is that the door is left unlocked and the evil one sneaks in unawares. Are you being as alert as possible?

Our physical front doors are often paired with another door. There may be either a storm door (that is basically a glass door that can be opened to let in sunlight), or a screen door (that is basically a full screen to let in fresh air). These kinds of doors can be a benefit in other ways. I recall a certain family who had a son who began to drink beer. The wise parents would make the son breathe through the screen before they would let him in. The screen door acted as a protection to prevent the entrance of someone who was doing things contrary to family standards.

We parents are a lot like these doors. We are a closed door, a door that is ajar (or always open), a screen door, or a storm door. Let's look at them individually.

The closed door is definitely not something a parent wants to be. One major reason is that it is virtually impossible to be a closed door for your child's heart. The child has to help control this also, because even if you are doing your "guard duty" properly, the child must be on the same page with you or they will find ways to open their door to the evil that is lurking outside. We can do our parts, but only as we partner with our children. This is a team effort. That is why the heart of a child must be in tune with his parents. Children have learned to sneak around parents for years. (Not that *I* ever did that as a child, of course.) But we can't be a closed door. We must begin to allow our children to grow in the world with guarded opportunities. Parents cannot shelter their child forever, and we don't want to do so. Our goal is to train them to mature into adulthood in a normal, beneficial way.

On the other hand, you might have a door that is ajar—just slightly open—or fully open. This is a very dangerous door. When you walk by an open door, I'm sure you, like most people, just glance in as you pass by. We seem to think it is our right. Whatever the case, the door ajar is not a good option for a family. In many ways, is not even using the door for its intended purpose. It basically allows anything and anyone into the house. The parent in this case is probably more like the absentee parent. If you are a "door ajar" parent, you are allowing anything or anyone into your child's heart. Children's hearts are so brittle. They can be so easily crushed by the things that they experience.

The screen door is the door that has a filter in place to keep out the bad and yet allow some good. The screen door permits sunlight, fresh air, smells of nature, and sounds of life all around. A screen door is healthy for a house, but it is not odor proof or disease proof. Germs, bugs, and all kinds of unwanted creatures can get through a screen door. While it isn't bad for a house, is that the kind of watch we want to have over a child's heart? It pictures a parent who is only somewhat discerning. The screen door gives some level of comfort, but it is not really doing the job. Too much gets through as the parents leave discernment up to the child, and the child is infected by more than they realize through friends, music, television, and other areas of contamination. A screen door approach is not a good approach to parenting. Most children do not see the danger of a screen door. If we leave them to make this kind of discernment, they are going to fail.

Parents make a serious mistake in thinking that decisions made while the child is so young will not have a long-lasting effect on the child. I have heard parents who divorce claim that their children are so young they will get over it and move on. I beg to differ with them. Children's hearts are not to be taken lightly. I have seen the pain in a child's eyes last for years. I remember the one story a teenage girl told me. She and her dad were sitting on the floor playing a game of some sort. They were just talking when the subject of divorce came up. He asked what she would do if her parents ever divorced. Without even looking up from the game, this beautiful young lady scoffed, "Oh Dad, you would never do that." The girl trusted her dad so much that she did not even look up. Just a few months later, this man left her mom for another woman. I spent many hours with her after the separation and divorce. Years later, she was still in pain. No amount of counseling can erase the pain of such a wound in the child's heart quickly or easily.

The "E" Challenge of the Heart—Entrance

Don't assume the heart is not worth guarding to the fighting end. The heart you save may be your child's.

The door I would like to recommend for a family is the storm door. My wife has been asking for a storm door for our home for some while, and I, preferring to live cheaply, don't see the need for it. You see, I work out of my home office. As a matter of fact, I am sitting at my computer typing away right now. The front door is only about 15 feet away. I have made my case that I don't need it, since I am the only one home. She has been gracious enough to let it go. (When she reads this, however, she is going to give me a fit.) In most houses, storm doors are optional, but for the heart of a child, it is not simply an option.

First, let's talk about a storm door. How did it get that name? I went on the internet and could not find a suitable answer. The best that people stated was it was designed to help keep a storm out of the house. I guess that fits with the name! No family wants a storm in their house. No family wants the elements of a storm in their house. The cleanup after a storm is messy and often things are damaged and ruined forever. But how few are really guarding the heart of their children to keep the storms at bay! I have watched children faced with storms that parents could have prevented if only they had put the storm door in place. Children confront: second hand smoke storms, alcohol storms, pornography storms, unguarded visitor storms, step-family storms, illegal and abused drug storms, addiction storms, overwork storms, laziness storms, and a whole host of other storms. All of these are storms that, for the most part, the parents could have prevented from getting into the house. Yet either through neglect or just outright sinful behavior, they allow the storms into the child's heart. Now I am not trying to minimize the pain of the adult, but it is the children that most concern me in these storms. They are clearly the innocent victims, and parents need to remember that their decisions have lasting effects.

The Old Testament talks about the sins of parents passing on to succeeding generations. How sad. I remember one such illustration that clearly pictures just this fact. A young man was about to marry his beautiful fiancée. The night before the wedding, his "buddies" planned a stag party for him and invited a certain "lady" to attend to be the entertainment. Needless to say the young man indulged and went on to marry his fiancée the next day. Not long after, the couple found out that they were going to have a baby. How exciting! It was what they had always wanted and longed for. The time and day came and the baby was born, but it wasn't long before the parents noticed that the child had trouble seeing. They took their child to a doctor, only to find that their child was blind. Apparently, Dad had contracted a disease on that fateful night before the wedding and passed it along to his wife. It went undetected at first, and the baby was the true recipient of the sin.

Storm doors let in light but protect from the weather. You can see the storms raging on the outside (it's not a closed door), but they can't touch you or your family. Just as a house could use a storm door, parents we need to be the storm door to our children's hearts. These hearts are too easily harmed and scarred. They are brittle hearts that need a storm protector, and that is the role of the parents. Now I realize that some storms are good for us to face. Storms can make us stronger. They say the best captains are those who have weathered many fierce storms. True, but do not put your child in the way of a storm before they are prepared for the test. That is another reason why those early years are so critical.

The question of when to open the door must be answered by each parent. For what things, people, issues, and storms will you open the door for your family and children? Those are the kind of decisions that need to be made with much prayer and discernment. By no means should you allow yourself to believe that these things are not serious. I recall hearing about the wagon trails that were part of the early development of our country. Settlers deciding to move west for the lure of land, gold, or just a new experience would find the paths that others had taken before them. Muddy roads and thin wagon wheels would cause ruts in the paths. These ruts were often very deep and almost impossible to get out of. Someone even placed a sign: "Be careful what rut you get into. It may take you the rest of the way." The same is true with parenting. We get lazy and the routine sets in, and the next thing we know we are following a path that is very difficult to get out of. Intentionally guard the hearts (the entrance) of your children—don't ever leave it up to the world to do it for you!

Parents: stand at the door of your child's heart and be the one to choose what or who has access. God has entrusted this to you. Guard them with your life!

9

The "A" Challenge of the Heart—Attitude

HOW OFTEN WE HEAR someone say about another person, "They certainly have a bad attitude." We also hear, "Attitude will help you gain altitude" and "Attitude is everything." What does all this actually mean?

I believe that parents allow their children to develop negative attitudes early in life that help formulate sinful thinking in their teen and adult years. Sometimes, it is hard to address because it is simply funny. I remember one time when one of my children called me "butt head." She was way too young to even know what the words meant, and we also had no idea where she even heard the phrase before. Needless to say, we did not punish her, but tried to determine where she had heard it and if she had any clue about its meaning. The attitude behind the behavior was more important to us than the actual behavior. Now, I am not saying that things of this nature should go unpunished. But sometimes there is no easy solution or fix, and to punish simply to punish will not always correct poor behavior. What if God punished us every time we did something wrong? I am not sure any of us would want that. So we try to develop our own proper attitude in the situation and to do all we can to get behind and discover the attitude of the child.

While they are formulating their attitudes, it is very important that you do not let the world dictate "correct" behavior. I often hear parents say, "Well at least they are not doing drugs." Their point: I can accept some bad attitudes when I look at the big picture. It is like the college student who sent an e-mail to her parents. It went something like this:

> Dear Dad and Mom,
>
> I wanted to send you this to alert you to some things that are going on with me here at school. I am pregnant but will not get an abortion. Plus, I am not even sure who the dad really is. With all

the parties I have been attending, it is really hard to tell. Also, I might be addicted to heroin. Everyone here does it so much and it simply is easily accessible and enjoyable. And I won't be home this Christmas as all my friends are heading to a commune to let it all hang out. I hope you don't mind.

Love,

Delores

P.S. None of the above is true, but I did fail my physics exam.

A very clever approach to a difficult situation! What the child wanted to do was to diffuse the anger over the real by painting the unreal. Parents often do the same thing, frequently in the area of attitudes. Parents become negotiators of the more extreme over the mundane. But remember that the mundane can lead to bigger issues. You can suppress a behavior because you are bigger, stronger, or older, but you cannot suppress what is going on inside the heart. That is where the attitude blossoms into the maturity. That is where bad habits develop and that is where sin begins to take root. As Paul describes in Romans 7, there is a battle raging inside of us, and the winner is going to be the area that is fed the most. Even allowing small bad attitudes to exist and fester has the potential for long-term consequences. Just convince a kid soon enough that he is stupid, and watch that attitude settle in for years. I have even heard parents excuse their child in these areas by admitting that they were once the same way. By doing so, you have given your child a license to emulate your behavioral problems! Just because we might be an idiot does not give us reason to raise idiotic children. God is all about breaking the chains.

They say that attitude is half the battle, or as Yogi Berra would say, "Attitude is 90% and effort 50%." No matter where you slice the pie, attitude is a key component in the parenting process, and there is no room for a bad attitude. We often hear people's excuses: they are having a bad day; they got up on the wrong side of the bed; it is that time of the month; they are tired; they can't help it with all they have been through. Parents seem to feel that it is necessary to give the child some room for a bad attitude, and they accept bad attitudes as normal. Everyone has them now and then, right? Let me just make it clear: *parents should give very little room for poor attitudes and the resulting behavior problems.* Determine now to not tolerate a bad or ungodly attitude. I realize that it takes hard work to keep ahead of the game, but we have God on our side and we do not need to excuse poor parenting when we have been

The "A" Challenge of the Heart—Attitude

given all we need to be great parents. A moment of attention to a bad attitude can go a long way.

First, there needs to be some effort made to attempt to determine why the child has a bad attitude. There might be something that they are not telling you, and that the attitude is really the symptom of something much bigger. This is especially true if a bad attitude isn't normal for the child. You never want to discipline a child over the wrong issue. Maybe someone has hurt them in some way, and the bad attitude is really a cry out for someone to notice them. The attitude is still wrong, but it might be their way of exposing the hurt a little. If there is a more mundane reason, like lack of sleep, make sure your child gets proper rest and some down time. You're the parent, after all.

Second, if you can determine that the attitude is just that, a bad attitude, do not tolerate that behavior. Bad attitudes left to grow unchecked become major problems later on. Every parent has to decide what will most be effective. Does it require some form of discipline or withholding of privileges? I can't suggest exact discipline since that depends on the circumstances, but don't ever ignore it. Anger, for example, may require a cooling-down period, but sending them to their room too often becomes "out of sight and out of mind." Face it and respond in strength to the situation, letting the child know that this kind of behavior will not be accepted in your family. Follow up with them after the discipline and look out for it more intentionally from then on. Evaluate problems you may have been missing all along; check with their teachers or other adults with whom they interact. Proper information can help you see more clearly what may have eluded you before. The key is to intentionally follow up. They need to leave the conversation knowing that you will not tolerate their mindset. If it continues, put more concerted effort into the situation—maybe even meet with your pastor. A bad attitude is like cancer; if left to itself, it will poison the individual and might very well poison everyone around him as well. One bad apple attitude can spoil the barrel, as they say. And these kinds of kids can destroy any event you may try to enjoy.

Take, for example, a day trip and how it can be dampened by one bad attitude. You get up to go to a favorite park or event and one child does not care to go. You are firm that he will go anyway and warn him to straighten up his attitude. The other children are almost begging you to leave him at home for fear that the one will ruin it for the rest. It would be a mistake to leave that one home. This is a family day and he needs to be brought to a place where he stops making life about himself. How you go about that might be a challenge, but he must not be able to win the day. If he does, more days like that are coming. Be strong and courageous and accept the responsibility of being the parent, and do whatever is necessary to bring the child into a right frame of mind. Family must be family with everyone doing their part. Deal swiftly and early with anyone trying to disrupt your family unity.

While bad attitudes should be dealt with quickly, good attitudes can be as quickly praised. Be swift to notice when your child sacrifices her own desires for someone else, or when he cheerfully obeys directions. When their focus is on the negative, show them what a positive focus would be in that situation, and praise them for adopting it. Humility should always be recognized, as well. Positive reinforcement goes a long way toward cementing the worthwhile attitudes in a child, so don't neglect this important aspect of their heart!

I cannot tell you exactly whether something is a bad attitude or not, but I can give some clear indications of what is a good attitude. Here are several good attitudes that every parent ought to seek to develop in their children:

1. Selflessness—Unfortunately, self-centered thinking is all around us. This is one that is not going to be easy. But spot the self-focus and deal with it often and consistently. There is no room in family for selfishness. That is why Jesus says if we want to follow Him, we must "deny" ourselves.

2. Humility—Scripture speaks over and over again about God's thoughts towards the proud, and none of them are good. Just as pride must be noticed, humility must be modeled and taught. Pride is one in the list of things that God hates (Proverbs 6), and Scripture makes it clear that God resists the proud, but gives grace to the humble (James 4, I Peter 5). But I don't believe we want to focus on the pride issue. Instead, continue to highlight humility. Be cautious; don't overstate the humble act, or they may become proud, but use it as an opportunity to stress the importance of a child with humility.

3. Love—I can't say enough about this attitude. Love is all through Scripture, and Jesus came because of love. Our children need to be taught the necessity of love and how it can cover a multitude

of sins. "And now abides faith, hope, and love, but the greatest of these is love" (1 Cor 13:13). How can we not do all possible to instill this in our children?

4. Serving—My dad modeled a servant's heart for me by taking care of several widows in our community. I often was dragged along, but now I cannot stress enough how valuable those images are in my mind. Even now I can see him, after a full day's work, bringing wood in to a lady who had no family and no way to take care of herself. It may be part of the reason I was open to the call of pastoring. Children need to develop a heart of service. You can do that through mission trips, serving in the church, or simply serving in the home.

5. Thankfulness—It is greatly concerning to watch a generation of "ungrates" today. I love to hold doors for people in public places just to watch their responses. It is truly sad to see how few are even appreciative. Teach your children to say, "please," "thank you," and other words that express appreciation and respect. A generation that has everything and believes that they are entitled to most will not learn to be appreciative for what they have.

6. Prayer—Although prayer is more than an attitude, it seems to fit best here. Children who are taught the attitude of prayer will find themselves more on their knees. Prayer helps keep their other attitudes in proper check, as it is hard to have a bad attitude when you are in His presence.

7. Commitment—Children should learn early on what it means to commit and keep their word. It is an attitude of respect and responsibility. We live in a day where man's word means so little. Let our children break that cycle and be a generation where once again man's word is more than just words, but is also his commitment.

I am sure that there are others that you may believe are essential. I probably would agree. The point is that we should do all we can as parents to deal with negative attitudes and instill upright ones. These attitudes at an early age will shape their adult years and cause their effectiveness for the King to either be diminished or enhanced. Does that not make it worth the time?

10

The "R" Challenge of the Heart—Relationships

HAVE YOU EVER CONSIDERED how easy this world would be if you did not have to deal with people? They are everywhere. They reside under your roof, work alongside you, live next door to you, and even attend church with you. They are all around you. And unless you plan on living as a recluse, you are going to have deal with people time and time again. Dealing with people means developing relationships, and those relationships are going to have an influence on you, whether good or bad.

I can still remember the many people in my life who have profoundly influenced me. My parents and siblings had the greatest impact. Then it was my grandparents who lived two houses down the street from me. I tell people often that I think my grandfather was my best friend growing up. I would rather spend time with him that anyone else. Then there was my aunt and uncle who lived across the street. They were and still are very dear to me. But after that, who were the movers and shakers in my life? There was Miss Estelle who helped lead our youth group. She was a monument of love and grace in my life. Then there was the man who had a place of business nearby who had pictures of naked women on his wall, my first exposure to nudity. Then there was the young man who gave me more information about sex than I needed to hear. There were some peers whose language was certainly not something that I heard in my house. Also, there were teachers who gave me a star on my paper at school. But the key players in my life came much later in college where God truly used some of His choicest saints to greatly impact me. (I especially praise the Lord for Jim Schuppe, Bob Evans, Dave Shive, Curt Lowry, Tom Edgar, and Stew Brady. These are only a few of the many who deserve praise from me for their kind care in my formative years.)

The "R" Challenge of the Heart—Relationships

Overall, however, I was greatly impacted by my parents. Their guardianship over me included keeping an eye on my choices of friends and determining whom I could date (even coming to get me one time when I snuck out on them). They chose often and carefully for me, guarding my heart in ways that I was too stupid to understand. This guardianship, which they took seriously, enabled me to be fertile soil, so that when I went on to Bible college, I was someone the Lord could continue to mold. Why? My heart had been prepared and guarded, especially in the area of relationships.

There were homes I was not permitted to be in. There were places of business that I could not frequent. One such place was a local teen hangout. It was basically harmless, or at least that is what I thought. But my parents forbade me to be there; the place had pool tables and the kids gambled. I thought my parents were being overzealous, and I didn't like the prohibition. Other Christian kids could go, but not me. I remember one time that I disobeyed my parents and went there. I only stayed a short while and quietly slid home. My house was about three miles away, so I thought that I had pulled off the act. Unbeknownst to me, the hangout had a distinct odor. The attendee didn't really notice it, but those who came near you knew it instantly. When I walked into the house, my mom immediately smelled the distinct smell and I was busted. Why? Because my parents were the guardians over me and they were not going to take that lightly. At the time, I resented losing relationships because I did not attend those places or those kinds of parties. Today, I can say that I am the better man because of it. Later in life I came across a great sermon by G.D. Watson that fit me well:

> If God has called you to be really like Jesus He will draw you into a life of crucifixion and humility, and put upon you such demands of obedience, that you will not be able to follow other people, or measure yourself by other Christians, and in many ways He will seem to let other people do things which He will not let you do.
>
> Other Christians and ministers, who seem very religious and useful, may push themselves, pull wires, and work schemes to carry out their plans, but you cannot do it, and if you attempt it, you will meet with such failure and rebuke from the Lord as to make you sorely penitent.
>
> Others may boast of themselves, of their work, of their successes, of their writings, but the Holy Spirit will not allow you

to do any such thing, and if you begin it, He will lead you into some deep mortification that will make you despise yourself and all your good works.

Others may be allowed to succeed in making money, or may have a legacy left to them, but it is likely God will keep you poor, because He wants you to have something far better than gold, namely, a helpless dependence upon Him, that He may have the privilege of supplying your needs day by day out of an unseen treasury.

The Lord may let others be honored and put forward, and keep you hidden in obscurity, because He wants to produce some choice fragrant fruit for His coming glory, which can only be produced in the shade. He may let others be great, but keep you small. He may let others do a work for Him and get the credit for it, but He will make you work and toil on without knowing how much you are doing; and then to make your work still more precious He may let others get credit for the work which you have done, and thus make *your reward ten times greater when Jesus comes.*

The Holy Spirit will put a strict watch over you, with a jealous love, and will rebuke you for little words and feelings or for wasting your time, which other Christians never feel distressed over. So make up your mind that God is an Infinitely Sovereign Being, and has a right to do as He pleases with His own. He may not explain to you a thousand things which puzzle your reason in His dealings with you, but if you absolutely sell yourself to be His love slave, He will wrap you up in Jealous Love, and bestow upon you many blessings which come only to those who are in the inner circle.

Settle it forever, then that you are to deal directly with the Holy Spirit, and that He is to have the privilege of tying your tongue, or chaining your hand, or closing your eyes, in ways that He does not seem to use with others. Now, when you are so possessed with the living God that you are, in your secret heart, pleased and delighted over this peculiar, personal, private, jealous guardianship and management of the Holy Spirit over your life, then you will have found the vestibule of Heaven.[1]

Accept it now, parents; you influence your children directly and you must guard them tenaciously. People impact people. If you don't believe that, ask yourself why God had to become a "people"? Why did He leave the greatest message ever in the hands of people? Why are there at least

1. G. D. Watson, Faith, Prayer, & Tract League Tract #76; Grand Rapids, MI 49504.

30 different "one another" statements in the New Testament describing how the members of the body are to relate to each other? Christians are commanded to love, pray, encourage, support, exhort, and bear one with one another. We are an interconnected people, and the question that Cain asked years ago about his brother Abel, "Am I my brother's keeper?" still resounds today. Yes, we are keepers of our fellow humans. Since that is true, we are very capable of influencing one another. Most people call it today by the phrase "peer pressure." It is still just as valid a concern as ever, and few on the face of the earth will not be influenced by it at some point in their lives. Peer pressure is people impacting people; if you don't control the people who impact your children, then the god of this world will take care of it for you. I recall my years as a teacher in high school watching the "newbies" (those who were new to the school and didn't know anyone), come off the bus and mingle in the crowd. It took very few days for the problem kids to congregate. How can they find each other so fast? You can move a child from school to school, and from state to state, but it won't change the results unless the child is changed. How do we change the child? We have to get the heart. I have seen the same in the body of Christ. Disgruntled members find each other.

This section is not an easy section to write. You see, there is a seeming paradox in parenting: the part where bad company corrupts good kids and the other part where every child is personally responsible for his/her own behavior. Both of these are true. Just because a child is in bad company does not mean that the child will do bad things. Yet unfortunately, bad company typically has an adverse effect on good children. You need to guard the heart of your child from any relationships that could be detrimental to their well-being and future development. Sadly, the list of potential people is long and varied.

Let me start with the most obvious: friends. Friends can be extremely important in the development of a child, both to the good and to the bad. Good friends (which, by the way, most children are unable to discern) can be such a blessing to your family. Just hearing that your child has chosen wisely can be so uplifting! And you can tell a lot about your child by the kind of children with whom they enjoy associating. Birds of a feather do flock together, and if your child continually chooses good quality friends, that is a good marker that they might be getting it right. Therefore, it is important to know the people your child is befriending. Many parents assume that if the child goes to church, Sunday School, youth, homeschool, or Christian school, then the child must be a good child. Not so fast. Those things may be controlled by the parents, and they may be only touching the child outwardly. Help your children discern what a good friend might look like, and help them choose consistently through that lens. Invite the friends in your home on occasions before just simply letting your kids go elsewhere. You can learn a lot about a child by having them in your home a few times. When they are polite, help with the clean-up, show respect in relationships, and the other things that you as a family deem important, you can begin to discern the quality of the friends your child has picked. I am not saying that there are only "good kids" and "bad kids." Perfectly "good children" may encourage negative traits in my kids. I want my kids to see that we are not the only family that has high standards. Unfortunately too many families, even Christian families, do not. You cannot choose too carefully. This goes into the dating arena, as well. For now, let me make it clear that extreme care must go into helping your child in the area of the opposite sex. Far too many parents take puppy love lightly. They are just kids today, but tomorrow when you wake up, you wonder where the years have gone. Even cute little crushes should not go unnoticed. Talk with your children about the selection that they are making because they may be giving you a hint later of what is to come. By no means allow your child to have a "date" with anyone outside of your eyesight if you are not fully confident in that person. Case closed. (More information on dating in Chapter 14.)

The power and persuasion of friends cannot be underestimated. Peer pressure and wanting to be accepted by the community is a strong force. If you do not control the community, the community will attempt to control your child. And since you cannot control the community at large, you can at least help control that which is the inner circle of your family. Help your children choose wisely, because the path is too dangerous for indiscriminate relationships. You don't ever want to put your children in a place where they have to choose between their friends and their parents. If they have come to that place already, you may have been shocked at the decision they made. So, do everything possible to keep them from making that choice, and you do it by keeping a close eye on their friends. Ask questions of those who may know the family and get to know them yourself. Are they active in church? Are they a

The "R" Challenge of the Heart—Relationships

solid, committed Christian family? Who are their friends? God wants you to make informed decisions about your children's relationships. Do not leave this up to them.

Another area of relationships concerns the family—closely connected family members; grandparents, aunts, uncles, and extended family—anyone who may show up at the family reunion, including in-laws and out-laws (which every family unfortunately has). There is a reason that Scripture says you are to leave father and mother and cleave to your wife. You need to do all you can to protect the ones that God has left into your care, and that protection even extends to protection from those in your own family.

If you have kept informed about the abuse situations that are in the world around us, you will know that most abuse comes from those whom the child knows, and unfortunately, it happens under your roof and by a - you guessed it - a family member. How did it happen? Obviously, the parents never suspected Uncle Zeb would ever do such a thing. That is how these predators get away with it. They are the people least likely to generate suspicion, and you, being naïve, give them the wonderful opportunity to prey on your children. How many parents out there are now kicking themselves for being so trusting? How nice of Uncle Zeb to help teach my girl how to drive a car! How kind of the cousins to offer my kids a ride! How sweet of the older stepchild to take my son under his wing!

I am not trying to put a wedge into the family, nor am I trying to put doubts in your minds about every member of your family. But the facts speak for themselves, and I would certainly put you on high alert about anyone who is allowed unsupervised access to your children. We live in a sinful world with sinful people doing sinful things daily. The news broadcasts daily information about another case that shocks us. How many more events need to occur before you begin to take guardianship over your children more seriously? It only takes one event to put a long-term scar on your child's heart, and also a scar on your heart that you will have to live with forever. I can hear someone say, "You are too paranoid." You can think whatever you want about my decisions to guard my children, but when I held them in my arms in that hospital room, I was given a gift from God, a gift that I take very seriously. I will one day answer for how I have guarded the hearts of my children. I would love to hear, "Well done thou good and faithful servant" (Matt 25:21). I don't want to have regrets on that day. What you want to hear that day is your choice.

I close this section with one final appeal to keep close eyes on those who have access to your children. I am a strong proponent of true Christian education. I make no apologies for that, but if you believe God would have you to choose public education, then I just want to again caution you greatly. You had better know what your children are hearing on a daily basis. Satan believes in the gradual decay of a heart, and he is patient enough to give it time to work. He loves to plant a seed here or there and wait for it to sprout. He loves to slowly chip away at the heart's defenses. Even if the odds are stacked against him, he does not mind a gradual infiltration of erroneous thinking. Generations are not conquered through isolated battles but long-term aggression. Communists boast that if you give them your children, they will one day control you. Be on guard against those to whom you are "giving" your children.

Oh, the beautiful heart of a child. On the sonogram in the mother's womb, you see that heart; they say you can detect a heartbeat now at 18 days and in some cases, even earlier. That heart is developed with all the rest of the parts of that beautiful child by the hands of a loving God who makes all things good. Then the child comes into the world and is entrusted into the hands of loving parents. Do not take lightly the protection of your children. God does not take lightly the watch over you, and nor should we.

An older hymn has had special meaning to me over the years. The title of this song is "Day by Day," written in 1865 by Berg and Ahnfelt. Look at the second stanza of this great song:

> Every day the Lord Himself is near me,
>   with a special mercy for each hour;
> All my cares He fain would bear and cheer me,
>   He whose name is Counselor and Power.
> The protection of His child and treasure
>   is a charge that on Himself He laid;
> "As you days, your strength shall be in measure,"
>   this the pledge to me He made.

I am not able to give my children the pledge and fulfill it as my God is able to do for us. But, I can still give it my all. I may fail as a friend of others, as an employee of my boss, as a citizen of a country, as a member

The "R" Challenge of the Heart—Relationships

of a church (although I don't want to do any of those), but I cannot fail as a parent. I must, for the sake of my kids, finish well. Their hearts depend on me to do so, and I cannot let them down. The protection of our child and treasure is a charge that we parents ought to accept. Yes, our God is there, and because of Him, we have great confidence in our chances of winning the battle. But we dare not take it casually. Falling asleep at the wheel in the relationship area is an accident waiting to happen.

11

The "T" Challenge of the Heart—Training

THE LAST SECTION ABOUT guarding the hearts of our children concerns the issue of the training of the child. I want to focus on three areas: the home, the church, and the school. There are certainly other areas of training, but these are the big three. I hope and pray that you will take these thoughts to heart and consider carefully that training that your children will receive.

I have watched a few episodes of a show that explains how Navy Seals are trained. They don't tell us everything about their training, but they make it clear that these men are far out of my reach. If you want to be part of one of the best special forces out there, this might be the training for you! But here's the point: you typically only get one chance to train well. Those who get the correct training have the best chance to succeed. How can Harvard and Yale and schools like that charge astronomical tuition and know that people will pay it year after year? They claim to offer the best, and for the best, no price is too great. How much more should we determine to give our children the best? Of course, I am not talking about extravagance. Giving our best might not be the same as someone who has unlimited resources, but God did not give our children to those parents. You probably have limited resources, so give them the best within that limit.

The Home

Let's begin with a discussion regarding the home and training. As I said earlier, this training ought to begin before conception and continue throughout years the child is under your care, whenever that is (especially since more kids are returning from college with bills and need to stay at home). For example, reading to them every night from

The "T" Challenge of the Heart—Training

properly-selected books will give them a love for reading. You should see our family at the beach. It is actually funny. We are an athletic family; all our children have been on the all-conference team or all-tournament teams; they have even been MVPs of tournaments. But when given a few hours or rest and relaxation, like at the beach, you may see six people with books in hand. Our children's love for reading began before they were born.

Give them educational tools that will enhance their learning and their fun. All work and no play is not the best policy, but neither is all play and no work. You can combine both in the home educational process. There are many excellent tools out there that are simply too numerous to cite. Just talk with your friends and do your homework and you will find exceptional materials that will help your children on their level. Although it might seem like the diaper era lasts forever, it does not. It won't be long until you are sending them off to college! Take time during those early years to give them proper development and training so that their hearts grow and mature in godly increases. Make learning fun and they will continue to desire it.

I am not going to fully address the issues surrounding the woman going back to work. Scripture teaches that women are to be "keepers at home" (Titus 2:5), but it does not say that they are to be "barefoot, pregnant, and in the kitchen." I believe that each family has to decide what exactly this verse means. Some believe the wife should not work outside the home and some do. Here is the overarching principle: if the wife cannot be a keeper at home and work outside, then something has to change. The overriding principle needs to be the home. As Abraham Lincoln said so well, "the hand that rocks the cradle is the hand that rules the world." In this economy things are tough for all families, and I am not trying to set absolutes beyond Scripture. But Scripture does say that the woman is to be the keeper at home. Now dads certainly can and should help around the house, and so should the children. But the Scriptures give the oversight of the home to the woman. If she is able to do that, however their family measures it, and can work outside the home, then I believe the freedom is there. Which leads to the next concern; what to do with the children?

If you decide that some form of day care is right for your family, I have one caution: choose wisely. How soon should a mom go back to work? Who should be given the privilege to watch little Johnnie? These are all very difficult questions that should not be answered by someone who does not know all the extenuating circumstances. Here are several thoughts to consider:

1. When you get married, learn to live off one income. That way if the wife gets pregnant, you have the option to keep her at home with the baby since you have been living off one income already. That would mean do all you can to get health insurance through Dad also, and avoid being financially driven through the discussion.

2. If going back to work is what you believe God desires for you, then consider working at home and part time as a first option. They grow up so fast.

3. If you choose someone to watch your child, do it with much prayer and counsel. Economics should *not* drive the decision, no matter how practical it seems. First look for someone you know personally extremely well to watch your child. This could be a family member or friend, but do your homework. Don't make assumptions and don't act hastily. This person may watch over your child many hours per week. That is a long time of influence and input into the early years.

   a. Put together some things you want your children to be given during those hours. You pick out the books, the movies, the educational resources. Do your homework well and expect the caregiver to use these materials. If you cannot do it yourself, you should at least be instrumental in what they do receive. Do not let them have all the play time while you are left with the harder work. Also, be sure you tell the caregiver what you expect in the form of correction. You are the overseer and the caregiver is simply a facilitator. If they do not carry out your demands as you request, then they should be replaced. My wife worked during some of our children's early years, but she set out the schedule and made sure those details were carried out.

   b. If you need to go with the daycare option, try to at least put your child in a daycare center that is Christian-owned and operated.

4. Dad must step up the help at home if Mom goes back to work. Too many men expect their wives to work, take care of the kids, the home, and them, while they golf, hunt, fish, or whatever. Shame on you, Dad. If your wife must work, pitch in and help so that the family can function the best way possible for God's Kingdom. You may have to put the clubs, the guns, and the fishing equipment away till later years. Men, do not permit your wife this burden without shouldering it as much as you can. She is expected to give more and so are you.

While I have not covered every scenario, this section will hopefully trigger good discussion and serious prayer about the guardianship of your children's hearts. These children did not ask to come into your home, they were given to you by God. Now go and guard them well.

The Church

The next area of discussion in training concerns the church. Before becoming a pastor, I was a member of several churches depending on where God had placed me either in my work or education. I have seen a number of different forms of churches and have certainly read much on this subject. One thing I've discovered along the way is that the educational component of a church should not be optional for the family. If you attend a church where there are few educational opportunities for your family, consider talking to the leadership about your concerns. It may also mean that you will need to change your place of worship. Admittedly, far too many families church hop, and far too many families decide on a church for the wrong reasons. But if a church does not have some good educational paths for your child, such as AWANA, Sunday school, or similar options, then you may need to help begin them or go to a church that has them.

Godly teachers with godly curriculum can be an extremely helpful asset to you and your family in the formal training of your child. But again, don't make assumptions. Find out what they are learning and get to know their teachers. Indiscriminately dropping your child off in a Sunday school class or any part of the church is not wise, and knowing the teachers, curriculum, and classmates is not out of the question. I would also want to know who substitutes when the teacher is not there and who oversees the ministry. Again, the responsibility of the child is yours, not the church's. You must do your part well.

Some families question whether Sunday school, junior church, or other things are worthwhile since they are segregated by age or sex or because they separate families. While I have not personally seen examples of families who choose one option being better or worse off than those who choose the other, I respect the decisions of each. Remember that God gave you these children and will hold you personally accountable for the route you choose for your family. Make the decision prayerfully and be the best for your child as you can. You are the guardians of their hearts. One word of advice from a pastor, however – do not allow your children to disrupt the worship or teaching in progress. Even nursing children can be quite a distraction; members and teachers who are uncomfortable with the process will focus a lot more on the nursing mom than on the teaching. I encourage nursing moms and parents with restive children to sit in the back or go to a quiet room where the service is piped in. This allows everyone to concentrate!

The School

If you think the previous topics are controversial, try having a conversation with people about the education of their children. You may need to put the gloves on! But considering the strong impact the educational process is going to have on your child, you'll need to be absolutely sure that you're doing the right thing for him or her. Schools have:

1. A social and spiritual influence. The students your child sees day in and day out will impact them socially and spiritually.

2. An intellectual influence. They way your child perceives the world and how it works will be largely shaped by what he or she is taught in the classroom each day.

3. A moral influence. Your child will be spending his or her most alert, concentrated hours with people who have certain morals and standards. Because children are sponges, they will absorb those standards—even older children do this. What will your child be absorbing?

Option 1: Home Education

In the last 15–20 years, home education has become rather popular. There are many reasons for that. For some, public education just is not an option and the cost of private education makes it hard for them to go that route. Others have been convinced by God that this is the best path for their family. Parents may also have motives such as the health needs of a child, geographical issues, job transfers, and a host of other reasons that are certainly worthwhile. I have known many families that have home educated their children very well. Many pioneers championed the cause of home education when it was neither popular nor socially acceptable. Today, although there is still some stigma associated with home education, for the most part it is accepted. And there are good reasons for that: for those who educate this way and do it with great precision, the children are excelling. It is hard to argue against a good product. A home educator's best advertisement is the product (the child) that they are producing. Undoubtedly, it would be incorrect to suggest that all those who home educate are doing a great work. To simply put all home education under the umbrella of success is not accurate. Yet, to allow the few to dictate the report of the majority is not correct either.

A few words of advice for those who home educate: First, be sure that God is calling you to do this. I say it is a calling because it is going to require a lot from you and your family. There are certainly plenty of benefits such as controlling the schedule, curriculum, and overall agenda, but there are also components that must not be overlooked. You need to know that this is what God has called you to do. Parents just need to keep listening to the Lord. He may have you take the child all the way through to graduation. He may have you put the child in some form of school the following year. Let that be His decision and not yours.

Second, be sure you understand the commitment required. Educating a child is a serious responsibility and should not be taken lightly. It will require your time, energy, and research so that you can offer a balanced view of the issues. In many senses of the word, in order to educate well, you will probably have to educate yourself. I realize that if God is calling you, then so what? It has to be done. I agree, but I still believe you don't want to undertake this kind of commitment without careful thought and prayer.

Although there are many who attempt to argue from the Old Testament that home education is the Biblical model, I strongly disagree. A case can certainly be made for home education from a number of key passages, but it is not accurate to say that it is the *only* way mandated in Scripture. To argue that you are convinced it is right for you and your family is certainly permissible and acceptable. Once you believe God has called you to do it, you ought to go after it with full passion.

One word of caution as we close this section. There are some families who say that the education of their children is their ministry and they are not able to serve in some capacity in the local church. Some even choose a church that is made up only of those who home educate. I believe that these are both false understandings of home education and the local church. Just because you home educate does not give you the privilege to stay away from church or to make church all about home education. The body of Christ requires us to be active and utilizing our spiritual gifts. No gift is for personal self-edification, and even if you believe your family is your ministry (which you cannot support Biblically), to make that your sole ministry is somewhat self-serving. God has called the church (not the family) to change the world. I understand that families make up the church, but the emphasis needs to be kept on His priorities. Don't lose your family for the sake of the church, but don't lose your church for the sake of your family as well.

I personally believe that home education is a good choice for some families. If God has called you to do it, do it well and raise up a generation for His glory. But even in doing so, please go after their hearts. Just because you educate at home does not mean your child's heart is in line with yours or the Lord's. Cultivate well and you will enjoy the benefits for years to come.

Option 2: Public Education

Public education is a difficult education to properly analyze for several reasons. One, it is free. Free education is appealing. I know that there is no way to measure it, but I wonder if private education was free, would it matter to you? Another reason is that it is convenient. Most students are picked up and dropped off within minutes from their door

The "T" Challenge of the Heart—Training

step; convenience also makes it hard to grasp the full impact. Another important reason is the facilities and programs. Very few non-public educations can compare with the government schools. Most children have many friends who attend public school. It is hard to go against the majority. Besides, parents say, if you pulled all the Christian kids out of public education, who will reach the rest? Also, Daniel lived in godless Babylon and came out 10 times better. Public education definitely seems to be an easier choice.

But I would like to challenge those who have simply assumed that public education is right for their children to pray right now before reading the rest of this book. Would you ask God to make the next few pages come alive to you and open up your reasoning, if you are not seeing clearly? If after reading and examining these pages, you are still convinced by God that public education is right for your family, then the discussion for me is over. You gave it to God and He led you accordingly. All I am asking is that you would look at this one more time. Fair enough?

In the next section, I am going to give my reasons as to why I believe Christian education (either schools or home education) are the only options for Christians. We can agree to disagree and I am willing to trust that it is the Lord that gave you the children and you are only accountable to Him. I just want to offer my counsel and sincere advice. Here are the concerns public education generates:

1. God and the Bible were clearly put out of public education by order of the Supreme Court back in the early 1960s. Yes, many believing teachers, coaches, and principals have done clever things so that they could to keep God in the classroom in some small way. And I know that there are laws on the books that actually protect believers more than people realize, but these do not change the facts. God and the Bible have been asked to leave by the authorities over public education. Do you think God takes that lightly? Do you think that there are consequences from that decision? Do you think God left? I believe God honored their request and public education in our country has statistically been on the decline ever since. The American College Testing Program did a survey that produced alarming results: seventy-six percent of American high school graduates would not be ready for even the basic first-year

college courses.[1] Yet our country was once the leader in education!

2. Secular humanism is today the god of public education. If you are not familiar with secular humanism, relativism, situation ethics, and other similar philosophies, then you might want to take some time to read up on these godless ideas. Public education today is built on the foundation of these systems, which are all anti-God and anti-absolute truth. If the foundation is rotten, how will the building hold up? The curriculum of the public education is steeped on the doctrines that are contrary to a believer's view of life. Read the books for yourself (most school systems make their curriculum available for parents). Don't you think reading and studying these books for hours each week will have a negative impact?

3. The majority of teachers, principals, coaches, school board members, and others who have leadership role in the school are non-believers. Now, just because they are non-believers does not mean that they are evil people. But, do you want non-believers to invest in your children six to eight hours every day? That, by the way, is more "quality time" than you will have with them in an average day.

4. The majority of the kids are not believers. Of course, Christians today will state that the public school is a great breeding ground for evangelism, and I agree. But what makes you think that your child is able to be that voice crying in the wilderness? Typically, godless environments drag down the godly, not vice versa. Your child may be the exception, but do you want to take that chance? And there are other ways to reach kids in public school without sending your children there as missionaries. (Young Life is one great work that is doing just that).

5. The majority of extra-curricular activities will be led by non-believers and will be greatly instrumental in shaping your children during the after-school hours. I can still remember my high school coaches and my respect for them. Do you know for sure that your child would stand against a respected teacher/coach if they admired that person? Is it worth the risk?

---

1. Joel Klein, *Atlantic Magazine*, June, 2011.

The "T" Challenge of the Heart—Training

6. There are alternatives that will provide everything a family needs for the education of their children. It is one thing to struggle with a decision when the options are not there, but that is rarely the case.

7. Government schools do not believe they have the responsibility to inform you of all the details involving your children. As you know, they can take your child to an abortion clinic without your consent. Government schools believe they know better for your children and could very well withhold information from you if they believe it is in the best interest of the child, or if they feel it is in the best interest of their "system" not to say anything.

8. Humanistic teaching begins in pre-kindergarten, and will be taught every year after that. Some may believe it is harmless, but many believe it is so serious that they will spend many hours, much energy, and a great number of resources to offer an alternative to combat the onslaught of humanism. May the Lord guide you as you shepherd His little ones.

Before I leave this area, let me again remind the parents that these are your decisions that you make on your knees in the presence of your Savior. I am not saying that God, for some reason not clear to me (and which He does not need to make clear to me), has given you the freedom to choose public education for your children. That is a decision between He and you. I will leave it there for you to discern.

Option #3: Christian School Education

Earlier in my ministry I wrote a position paper on why I chose Christian education for my children. All four of my children have attended Christian schools and have graduated from Christian schools. We home educated our oldest daughter for one year in the 9th grade, but other than that year, we have chosen Christian school education. While there is some repetition of the things we have already discussed, I wanted to share part of that paper with you so you know the heart of our family. I pray that you will examine these thoughts on your knees and in His presence.

> First, notice the title of *Christian Education*. *Christ* is the spelling of the first six letters in the word for the education called Christian education. It is named that intentionally. Yes, there are Christians teachers, staff, and children at government schools,

but can you openly share your faith and attempt to convert others to it? Can the Bible be used as a textbook? Can assemblies have pastors explaining the Gospel? Can you give the message at graduation about what Jesus means to you? I want my children drawn to as much Christian influence as they can get. Government schools cannot do this for my children. Paul says to follow him as he is a follower of Christ (1 Corinthians 11:1). That is what an educator must be doing.

Second, I believe it is important to compare the teachers. At the Christian school, the teachers are all equipped and trained to be educators. Some have master's degrees or are working on them. Many Christian schools in our area have received accreditation from the American Association of Christian Schools and Middle States Association (secular). Qualified, degreed, and dedicated teachers are serving in Christian schools. (Be sure to check out the Christian school first. Do not assume they are all the same.)

But even beyond that, Christian teachers meet every morning with the Savior and read His Word and then prayerfully come full of the Holy Spirit to interact with your children. Give me a Spirit-filled man or woman to lead my children and then I believe I have the more qualified teacher. Education is not simply facts, books, and information. Education is about living. If a man or woman knows their subject well, but lives a life contrary to truth, are they really the best choice to be an educator over my children? I can tell you without question, I will take a Spirit-filled teacher any day over whatever expertise a government school can offer.

It is also important to note that these teachers believe they have been called by God to this ministry. That certainly adds a deeper dimension to why they do what they do. They also take seriously the call to mentor our children. These are not just educators. These teachers are investing in God's kingdom. I want Christian role models for my children. Paul also warned that if anyone preached any other gospel other than that of Jesus, they were to be accursed (Galatians 1:8). We need to be sure what Gospel is being preached wherever our children attend. By the way, humanism is a false gospel.

Third, let's discuss curriculum. If you examine a history or science textbook in a government school, what is conspicuously absent? I have never seen a government textbook that gives God His rightful place. They espouse evolution, a history without a God who works all things according to His will, and a future view with no concept of Jesus' return. Do you believe that years of exposure to this kind of propaganda with their champions preaching their godless cause every day will not have any effect on your children? Insulation is one thing, but overexposure is another. Will children in Christian schools all turn out right and children in government schools all turn out bad? Of course not. That is not my point. I am only responsible for my children and I can see no educational reason for them to attend a government school.

Wisdom begins with the fear of God (Proverbs 1:8) yet many government schoolteachers have no fear of God. What is the source of their wisdom? I do not want those who are humanistic and have written textbooks with their agenda to be the steady diet of my children's learning. Christian school curriculums both educate and keep God in his rightful place.

<u>Fourth</u>, I send my children to Christian schools because I want the greater opportunity for them to be challenged, taught, and discipled by people of like faith. My children see their teachers and principals on Sunday with their Bibles in their hands. They know that these teachers have sacrificed to teach in a Christian school. It is more than a job to them. They have elementary teachers who still keep in touch with them. Our children serve in church with some of those teachers in junior church and other ministries.

Christian education is not a choice for our family. It is who we are. I believe this education has given our children the best potential to grow in wisdom and stature and in favor with God and man. It is the same way the child Jesus grew (Luke 2:52). If a government school can do a better job with this passage than a Christian school, you have my blessing. Jesus told us in the great commission to go into all the world and make disciples. If we choose twelve or so years for our children that does not enhance that process, are we missing out on the greatest call for our children? Although Christian education has its faults, it is a far superior path for our Christian family than what the government has to offer.

I would be remiss to not at least mention that there are a few unique situations that Christian schools presently do not accurately address. One such situation would be children who learn differently. Some Christian schools have special needs education, but not all do. That makes it hard for families in these situations. And if a family believes that they cannot teach this particular child at home, then government education may be the only option. Another situation might be if there is no Christian school nearby. Of course home education can certainly work for a family in that scenario, but if they don't believe home education is for them, maybe public education is the only choice. Make it prayerfully. I am not a proponent of sending the gifted and talented to public schools, nor the better athletes. You can get extra education and sports opportunities by utilizing other ways to supplement your child's abilities if the Christian school does not offer enough. In sports, for example, there are numerous Amateur Athletic Union (AAU) teams and travel teams that permit the exceptional athlete to get more competitive, if the Christian league cannot. By the way, many college coaches use those games and leagues to recruit for their institutions. Through AAU our daughter received many calls and contacts.

So, can a Christian family send their children to the government schools? That is a question that every family must personally decide. There are no Biblical commands stating that it would be sin to send your children to these schools. I also strongly teach that this is a decision each family must make. I believe it would be wrong to become involved in making this decision for other families. I have only given you reasons to examine on your own. In the end, would God actually lead a family to the public schools? It is possible, so I don't want to ever say exactly what God might do that is not clearly articulated in Scripture. There was a time (before separate Christian schools) when God likely was sending the majority of His children to the government schools, although that has probably changed since He was expelled! Therefore, I believe that if God does send a family to the government school it would probably be more of an exception, not the rule. But in the end, this must be a decision made between God and the parents, since those are the people He has entrusted with His gifts, His children. Dear parents, please make this decision with the clear leading of God, because I believe the government school is the exception for the Christian child, not the norm, and Satan is using public education to help destroy the hearts of our children.

Before leaving this subject, please let me add a few final thoughts. The purpose of this section has not been to offend or anger. I have only desired to give you food for thought. As believers we can agree to disagree. If you take these thoughts and pray more intently and be more on the alert, then it will be worthwhile. We live in a fallen world, and believers need to come alongside each other and worship and work

The "T" Challenge of the Heart—Training

together in spite of our differences. Let us not allow the education of our children cause division. We are one in Christ and that is always the most important stand that we can take. You decide. But be sure to do so on your knees and before His presence.

How Not to Choose

I especially don't want you to get an F on the education of your children. Therefore, I want to give you some of the normal motivators that families use to determine how to educate their child. The problem is, none of them *should* be used to make that decision. Interestingly, they all begin with the letter F:

1. Don't let finances control the decision. Do you believe God is able?
2. Don't let facilities control the decision. God does not dwell in buildings, but in people.
3. Don't let friends control the decision. Friends change, move, and can be a stumbling block to clear thinking.
4. Don't let family control the decision. Your children should not make this decision, and do not let others in the family make this decision.
5. Don't let fun control the decision. Sports, proms, dances, and all the frills can be alluring. Just ask the Biblical character named Lot who was drawn to the "thrilling" city of Sodom.
6. Don't let fame control the decision. The reputation of a school does not guarantee a heart after God.
7. Don't let fear control the decision. Who cares what others may say?
8. Don't let form control the decision. Programs can change overnight. And be sure to know the heart of the program. Don't read it from a distance.
9. Don't let fixations or location control the decision. The drive can be worth the ride.
10. Don't let flesh control the decision. Are you being led by the Spirit or flesh?

Summarizing Thoughts on Training the Heart

I doubt we will ever have full agreement on the proper methods, attitudes, actions, and behaviors of parenting. I also doubt that we will ever have agreement on the various forms of training in parenting. That is why there are so many options. But I would like emphasize the things that I hope we would agree on, and maybe these will help formulate your thinking as we close this chapter:

1. The education of our children cannot be taken nonchalantly. Eight hours a day for 13 years (excluding summer) is a serious investment of time. That amounts to roughly 17,680 hours that someone (and possibly the lost) will have to influence our kids. That decision must be made prayerfully.
2. The education of our children will affect them for the rest of their lives. How many of us remember the influence our educational years had on us? How many of us are not even aware that we do things today because of an educational event in our formative years? The amount of time and influence shapes us for life.
3. We will be held accountable for our choice for our children.
4. What we choose one year does not have to be the choice for every year.
5. Whatever choice we make, there should still be parental oversight, because we are ultimately responsible for our children.
6. We need to be actively involved in our children's education.
7. God loves these children more than we do and has a special plan for each child.
8. Children should be challenged to consider ministry over the world.
9. The years go by fast, so…
10. Choose wisely.

I would love to go back and do my parenting years all over again. Unfortunately, that is impossible. With all this information, I hope to spare you from regrets. Pray and seek His face as He reveals to you the training path for the children He has entrusted to you.

12

From Information to Transformation

SO FAR THIS BOOK has focused on the "why" of the heart with some scattered bits of advice and counsel along the way. This chapter is designed to go right after the heart of the issue (excuse the pun). While we may accept the ideas presented so far, we could become frustrated trying to understand how to bring them about. Hopefully, this chapter will help in that process.

Parents may wonder what the balance is between going after the heart and establishing rules and boundaries that control behavior. The answer can be found in Scripture as our Lord, as in all things, sets the precedent for us. God desires to go after our hearts, yet He also has given us rules and restrictions. In the Old Testament, they were called the Law, particularly including the Ten Commandments. The Law was only beneficial for those whose hearts already were turned towards Him. Laws without inward change are merely words. If God our Heavenly Father gave laws (rules and restrictions) to His children, why shouldn't parents?

In the New Testament, He commanded the disciples to go and make disciples of all nations, teaching them all that He had *commanded* them (Matthew 28:19–20). He even said earlier that they would be His disciples, if they kept His *commandments* (John 8:31). But with those rules came also the need to transform the heart. Rules, laws, and commandments have always been a major part of God's plans.

What Won't Work

I want to start with what will not work, because I consider myself truly an authority in this area. I don't want you to have to reinvent the wheel.

My mistakes, along with others that I have observed, will hopefully help steer you in a correct direction of truly going after the heart.

First, don't just make rules on the spot. Imagine sitting at the dinner table and little Sally spills the jelly. Dad immediately says, "From now on, no more jelly at the table." This is a rule made more out of frustration than consideration. The children read right through that. They know you are frustrated and they know the rule will not even stick. Dad has just weakened future rules by making this one in a moment of pique.

Second, don't make rules or consequences that you are not going to enforce. This is very similar to the previous directive, but these rules may have been made with thought and time. For example, a parent might assert, "If you are disrespectful to me again, you cannot speak for the rest of the day." You know that you have no intention of enforcing a rule like that, and it might even cause more problems later on when the child doesn't answer you! Avoid trying to fix the heart with harsh and rash statements that only inflame. Paul said it so well Ephesians 6:4: "Fathers, do not provoke your children to wrath."

Third, don't follow the old adage of "Do as I say, not as I do." Children are instantly aware of hypocrisy and are often driven away from the parent who requires things that they are not willing to do themselves. Parents who send their children to church and don't attend themselves send the wrong message. Their actions say, "This isn't important for your life, it's just another thing to keep you busy." If you don't want your children to do something, then make sure you set the right example. Years ago there was an amazing commercial on television from the American Cancer Society. I am not sure I remember all of the exact details, but I do remember the essential parts. A father and son were spending a Saturday together. They cut the grass together with Dad using a push mower and the little boy using one of those bubble blowing play mowers. Then they washed the car together, and the boy washed his little car. Then they sat down under a tree and drank a lemonade. After that, the Dad picked up his cigarettes and put one to his mouth, setting the pack down between them. Guess what the boy did? And how effective do you think the father will be when he tells his child, "Don't smoke. It's bad for your health"?

From Information to Transformation

What Will Work

First, and foremost, it is critical that you be a man or woman after God's heart yourself. It is very hard to lead that which you don't personally have. As the story above shows, children actually do want to model their parents. They have grown to learn your ways over their years of development and you have truly impacted them more than you realize. How many have said things like: "I never want to be like my Dad/Mom." Yet as they grow older, they find themselves doing many of the same things. The greatest gift you can give to your children as you attempt to draw their hearts to God is to have a heart yourself after God.

What does a heart after God look like? There are several key components:

1. Has a personal relationship with Jesus
2. Meets with God daily and on a genuine basis
3. Stays in close communion with God throughout the day
4. Walks in humility
5. Has a Kingdom view of the world (eternal values)

If these are the goals of the parent, then truly the children are going to see these qualities lived out in front of them. If they see this kind of living, they will see the benefits that go with a parent who has a heart after God. Not only will they see the heart in you, but they will see God's hand on you in ways that are not explainable other than God. This kind of faith is desirable faith. In general, our kids aren't really seeing enough of that. It is not that they have seen the faith and don't want it; I believe the problem lies in the fact that they are still looking for someone to demonstrate genuine faith to them. That must begin at home. Let your children see you in the Word. Let them see you serving in the church. Let them see you sacrificing for the Kingdom. Let them see genuine faith in action. Let them see Christ in you. That kind of faith and heart after God is extremely appealing. Is your faith appealing or distracting?

It is also very important that you ask forgiveness when you are wrong. I have not been the best at this, unfortunately. I have learned the hard way that a stubborn heart of a parent is not helpful in developing the heart of a child. I have often thought that being stoic and unmovable was more important than admitting wrong. Fortunately, my children have been very forgiving of this poor example in their father, but I am learning more and more of what it means to own your failures and admit you are wrong. We all sin and fail as parents and our children know it. Why do we think we need to be something we are not? Our phony façade will only drive the hearts of our children further from the Lord.

Finally, do make rules and restrictions that are positive. We teach our children early on not to touch the stove, not to put something into the outlets, not to play in traffic, and similar things. Teach them the purpose behind the rules and restrictions. Explain the punishment clearly and the consequences. If rules follow a heart after God and a forgiving spirit, you will be well on the way to helping your child become a woman or man after God's own heart.

But Why Are Rules Necessary?

But wait…if the heart is the issue, does that mean that there are to be no rules at all in a house? If we have rules, are we not just slapping a coat of paint on a house that needs the foundation fixed? Is this not hypocrisy?

No, this is not hypocrisy. I am not sure why we have concluded that to make a child behave in some fashion when their heart is distant produces a hypocrite. That is not what hypocrisy is. Hypocrisy is the example of the religious leaders in Jesus' day who drew near to Him with their lips but their heart was far from Him (Matthew 15:8). The hypocrisy was not them drawing near with an outward phony attempt, but also their belief in their heart that they were right with God as they tried to force laws on others that they were not willing to follow themselves. It is not hypocrisy to enforce rules or codes to keep a normal level playing field. Can you imagine football with no rules? Do the rules hinder the game? Of course not, but a football game with no rules would not be football. The same in parenting is true. There needs to be rules even if the child is not on the same page as you wish. To simply leave out rules and restrictions because the heart is not there is not wise. You are creating a lawless young person who will think life is similar when he becomes an adult. That is why many young people who have grown up with no rules often find themselves in trouble later in life. Rules are part of life.

The point is that you cannot use the rules *solely* to get to the heart. Rules have a place in the overall goal of getting to the heart, but rules alone will not produce a heart in the right direction. The rules of the Old Testament were simply made to prove how we cannot measure up without a renewed heart. That is why Jesus came to demonstrate grace to people who could not achieve righteousness by following the rules. Your children will also not be able to measure up perfectly, but with the goal of turning their heart with proper rules for life, there is no reason why the rules cannot be beneficial. Every family needs boundaries, rules, and restrictions, coupled with a desire to get to the heart of the child. We expected our children to be daily reading their Bible and praying. We taught them how to tithe. We expected them to be in church, even if they did not want to go. We had rules that we enforced on them, even though spiritually they were not always in the right place with God. That expectation does not produce hypocrites. It produces children who have learned that life is not about them and that God expects them to live both an outward life of conformity and an inward heart of allegiance to Him. The outward and the inward need to meld together.

Rules have become a bad concept in many Christian homes. Some parents think that they stifle the child, or they feel that the rules simply bring out sin. But the rules are necessary for the normal functioning of the home. Rules surrounding bed times, meal times, quiet times, television times, etc., really help bring about normal family structure. For example, television rules need to be established. We taught that during the school week, television was not permitted. Others give a certain number of hours per week to a child. Once those hours are used up, they can no longer watch television. It builds discipline and discernment and helps the children understand decision making and consequences.

Parents may need to evaluate the rules and responsibilities periodically. Some rules may need adjusting as the children grow older. Ten-year-old children may need to be in bed by 8 p.m., but children at 16 might be allowed a different time. It will be up to each family to make these rules prayerfully and carefully. I would also suggest you make them as a couple and present them to the children, explaining what you expect from each rule. Let them voice their concerns and be honest about the rules. But in the end, make the rules and stick with them. You are the parents, and they must understand your role to guard and oversee. No one said being a parent would be popular, but the benefits will be long lasting as you make rules to protect your children from the evil and evil one.

What Rules Accomplish

Every home needs rules to function properly—a home without rules is chaos. Whether or not a heart is changed, the structure must be in place. However, it is important to remember that rules without a heart change cannot produce godliness. The heart must first be led to Christ and then the rules help formulate a life that continues to be in favor with God. Therefore, rules are necessary both before and after salvation.

As to which rules you ought to have, that is up to you. But keep your goal clear: you must bring your child from information to transformation, then keep them on the path with rules so they can model this transformed life.

Part Three

Practical Application

This section is designed to help you take the previous chapters and put them into a practical form. It is my prayer that these chapters will stimulate both thought and action and help you become more intentional about your parenting in the day-to-day details.

Part Three

The Last April Moon

13

Some Important Must Do's For the Heart

IN THIS CHAPTER, I would like to give you some concise principles that I call the "must do's" of parenting. While there are other lists, these particular valuable items, gleaned from years of parenting and pastoring, are designed to help you capture and hold the heart of your child. I wish that I had a list like this when I began the parenting journey, and I wish that I had practiced all these in my parenting!

Avoid Child-Centered Parenting

I've said it before: avoid making everything about the child. We live in a child-centered world. Once the pregnancy is confirmed, the mad rush is on. We buy hundreds of books, spent countless hours immersed in the process, and the baby becomes all-consuming. While preparation is important, the danger arrives when the balance is lost. Research and preparation are important, but only the Savior needs to be all-consuming. The beginning often is a signal of things to come.

One of the first examples is the baby shower. Baby showers are both entertaining and beneficial. Most families can use the additional gifts from the showers—strollers, cribs, clothing, etc. In this economy, a little can go a long way. But the point is that the continued saturation makes the baby seem important above all else—in a way, that child is becoming a god of a sort. Add to this the many doctor's visits, the new clothes for the change in a mom's figure, the new diet, the vitamins, the exercise, the sonograms, and the shopping for "necessary" items, and you see that the baby has become the all-consuming world for the parents. Every phone call, every e-mail, every text is now about the baby.

I Heart Parenting

Please don't get me wrong. Too many children are neglected in our world and more attention needs to be given to the many "throw away" babies. It is sad when a world neglects its old and young as we do. But in the normal family, there is the danger of the baby god. There was only one Baby God, and He was the Son of God. All other babies are actually little sinners who have entered a sinful world and are in deep need of a Savior.

However, once the baby is born, that child-centered idea often gets worse. Expectant parents come to the hospital with porters to carry their cameras and film equipment, looking like tourists in downtown Paris. Some parents also want to video the entire birthing process. Now I don't want to sound too old-fashioned here, but there might be a reason that these kinds of images have remained in the confines of the hidden until recently! Years down the road, who will be watching this show? You can almost hear the new Dad talk: "Now here we are in the fourth hour of the delivery. Mom is doing well…. Scream for the camera, dear! Look at that doctor! He looks like a quarterback ready to receive the ball! Speaking of the ball, anyone know what the score of the game is? Oh, and there's Aunt Matilda, peeking in the crack in the door! Hold on there, Tillie—he hasn't arrived yet! Wait…there's a crown… yes, I think…I think it's a head!" And the play-by-play continues.

The baby is born and cameras begin to snap rapidly. Paparazzi can only imagine the photographic value of this red-carpet event. The camera clicks wildly, and within minutes, the happy dad has the baby posted on Facebook and all pictures go viral. With just a few clicks, this baby is world renown. And it is only going to get better. After Mom is cleaned up, with makeup on and hair brushed, the pictures continue: pictures of her holding the sleepy infant, pictures with dad and his son's first football, or maybe the new iPad (can't start them too young, can you?). Then comes the constant parade of family and friends—even the plumber who fixed the bathroom last week has to come by! Has a celebrity been born? Want to add more chaos? Have twins! People come to see the babies in procession, lining up as if they're seeing a three-headed child. (Can I just tell you that twins are simply two babies? Duh.)

Now the baby gets to go home. After the police escort, the family arrives home to the next phase of child-centered parenting. More visitors, more pictures, more gifts, more and more of whatever else that continues to make everyone believe that the world revolves around the

Some Important Must Do's For the Heart

baby. Again, please don't miss the point. Visitors, gifts, etc., are all very helpful. But please keep the Lord first in all that you do.

As the child grows, everything becomes centered on the "firsts": their first smile, their first laugh, their first spoonful of food, their first steps, and whatever else becomes the topic of discussion. And here comes the camera again. Everyone talks about what great promise the child shows! Parents often begin to brag that their child talked early, walked early, counted early, was ready for Kindergarten at age 2, threw a football the length of the field at age 4, and on and on *ad nauseum*.

Ok, so I have been rather cynical here, but I have stretched the picture to drive home a point. (Literally speaking, it's called hyperbole.) Basically, we make our children self-focused because we focus on them to the exclusion of almost anything else. As long as we continue down this path, self-obsession is going to be a constant battle with our kids. You would think our generation would contain the most confident kids around, but compared to earlier generations, you will find that our kids today just think that they are the center of the universe. How did they get there? Look in the mirror.

Positive Affirmation

After that lengthy tirade on child-centered parenting, it's important to add some information on positive affirmation. This important part of parenting begins and ends with the encouragement of love. Children need to be held, cuddled, snuggled, and loved. Children need to be affirmed. Children need to be told that they are loved. There was hardly a day that went by where I did not tell my children that I loved them, even if they were not doing what I wanted them to do. They needed to know that I loved them, not because of anything that they did or did not do, but because they were my children. This kind of love is the same our Heavenly Father gives to us. He loves us because He is our Father and we are His child.

There used to be a bumper sticker that you would see often when we were driving around any city or town. It read, "Have you hugged your kid today?" It was a great reminder that in a world of hate and hatefulness, children need to have a loving home to come to at the end of a day—a home where dads and moms love each other and love their children. I Corinthians 13:13 might be a great model for the family:

I Heart Parenting

"Now abides faith, hope, love; these three, but the greatest of these is love." Earlier in that same chapter (vv 4–8), Paul gives some specifics about love and how it looks:

1. Love suffers long.
2. Love is kind.
3. Love envies not.
4. Love vaunts not itself.
5. Love is not puffed up.
6. Love does not behave itself unseemly.
7. Love seeks not its own.
8. Love is not easily provoked.
9. Love thinks no evil.
10. Love rejoices not in iniquity.
11. Love rejoices in the truth.
12. Love bears all things.
13. Love believes all things.
14. Love endures all things.
15. Love never fails.

What would happen if every home practiced these verses in their family encounters? What if wives loved their husbands this way? What if husbands loved their wives this way? What if parents loved their children this way? What if children loved their parents this way? Can't we see that this kind of family relation would cause the family members to blossom and grow in ways beyond imagination? Jesus said that the greatest of all the commandments is summed up in love. And since most children learn via the models in front of them, maybe we need to examine more closely the love shown to them by their parents (or lack of love). If children grow up in a home where they are loved and affirmed, they will be more loving and affirming of others. Children need to also see that modeled within their parents' marriage. They also ought to have loving homes around them. Again, we are looking at the saturation mindset.

Some Important Must Do's For the Heart

As you can see, the struggle lies in the balance between affirmation and exaltation. Proverbs is clear: "Do not withhold good from those to whom it is due when it is in the power of your hands to do so" (Proverbs 3:27). Yet too much affirmation makes the child believe his own press releases. Dad will tell his son over and over that he is the best player on the team, and argue with the coach that his son should be out on the field during every play. Mom will demand that her daughter must move up through the competition levels because her girl is "clearly Olympic material." I have four children and I can tell you that as much as I love athletics, as much as I played many sports well in high school and college, not all my children share that same athletic prowess. For example, we signed our second child up for basketball in the town youth league when she was ten. Her older sibling had played around that age and it seemed like it was time. When we went into the gym for the first practice, I watched with wide eyes as the girls dribbled and passed the ball proficiently. After three minutes of observation, she and I went home and never returned. Any number of parents would have complained that I was damaging her self-esteem beyond repair, but I was actually saving it. I wasn't putting her in a situation for which she wasn't prepared. She never played basketball, but she went on to nursing school, excelled, and has been confident and cool in many more dire situations than a basketball game ever since. Her confidence came from not from doing the things she couldn't do, but from doing well in the things God had prepared for her to do.

You can see, then, that parents need to be realistic about their children's abilities and talents. Unrealistic affirmation leads to much pride and disillusionment. Too little affirmation leads to self-doubt and often despair. Parents need to see their children through the eyes of God. These are children made in the image of a loving God, and He has given them unique talents and features. When the Lord finished His original creation, the Bible states, "God saw that it was good." When God formed your child in the womb (Psalm 139), it was as if you could hear God saying after each loving touch, "It is good." After He put the heart in place, the eye coloring, the bone structure, and whatever else that makes your little darling unique, you could almost hear Him say, "It is good." And that includes all those that the world considers abnormal. Remember: God does not make anything abnormal. Every child is made in His image and His likeness, and they are good. Affirm your child daily and often.

I Heart Parenting

Give Them a Good Marriage to Observe

A sad statistic says that over half the children in the United States will watch their parents divorce, and half of those will also see the breakup of a second marriage.[1] And that does not take into account the many homes where parents stay together but the home is anything but loving. These kinds of homes take a terrible toll on the children. God helps these children rise above their circumstances, but never underestimate the damage that can be done in a home that is divided and distraught.

I realize that some situations are impossible to avoid. In those circumstances each family must get proper help from their extended family, friends, and local church. God can take that which the locusts ate and restore beauty beyond measure (Joel 2:25). But there are other situations that just ought not to be. One of those that most concerns me is the break-up of the Christian home. I am sure that very few, if any, young men and women who take vows before God in a wedding ceremony ever dream that they will divorce. Yet the statistics are high, and many families are crumbling. Parents need to make their marriage commitment, "till death do us part," actually mean something. Children did not vote to come into this world, and they did not vote to be in the middle of a disastrous relationship. Their dependence on their parents lasts a long time, and while step-parents have been very beneficial in many cases, there is rarely a better fit than the natural parents.

Therefore, I highly recommend marriage conferences, seminars, books, or counseling if necessary. Sit down with your pastor and discuss the issues that might be causing harm in your marriage. Far too often pastors are called when the wife is leaving or the husband won't come home. If you see conflicts rising and solutions elude you, seek help. Waiting until the final big explosion may just be too late. Our pride keeps us from seeking help earlier, but we must die to that pride and remember that "God opposes the proud, but He gives grace to the humble" (James 4:6). Plan dates. Talk with one another often and regularly. Do things together. Just love on each other and watch how kids blossom in your home! I will admit that I have not been the perfect husband. My pride and self-focus has often caused heartache in our home. Fortunately, God's grace prevailed and our marriage is the stronger today. To God be the glory, and thanks to a very patient and never-quitting wife.

1. "Children and Divorce Statistics," children-and-divorce.com, 2012.

Some Important Must Do's For the Heart

When I am right with God and love my wife, things in our home are much more smooth and enjoyable. You would think that since I know this, I would be on top of my game 24/7. It doesn't happen! But, with God's grace and a family's mercy, we are moving closer every day. A loving family provides the best life possible, and goes a long way toward developing a child who is equipped as God wants him to be.

Make Church a Priority

I know that this may sound self-serving, being a pastor, but I have seen the benefits over the years of being an active part of a strong, Bible-believing church. I don't want to make this about doctrine, denominations, music, color of carpets, stained glass, or whatever else may cause someone to become a church hopper. Find a God-fearing Bible based church, join, get involved, and make a difference. Be an active member, not just one who happens to be on the church roll. Let your children see you are committed to the local church and don't allow sports, personal activities, and pleasures to continuously erode this commitment. Missing church periodically for an event of some sort is certainly not sinful, but the pattern of missing church often for world things can send a message to your children that God comes last in your life. Not a good path to travel.

Regular church attendance can have many benefits. Studies from the Barna Research Group, Duke University, the *American Journal of Sociology*, and several others have documented the benefits of regular church attendance. For example, children who attend church regularly:

- Are less likely to get into trouble at home or at school.
- Argue with their parents less (and what parent wouldn't like that?)
- Rebound from depression faster
- Are more likely to be diligent workers
- Are more likely to succeed in school.

With all those benefits, why would anyone think going to church would be a waste of time?

In conjunction with this, I would also strongly suggest that you make every effort to stay in the local church. Do all you can to not hop from church to church. There are times that leaving a church is necessary. But, if at all possible, make your membership at the local church a high priority, and attend consistently. Even pastors have the desire to stay home from church now and again; I'm prone to it, too, even after 26 years. Along those lines, I remember hearing a story about a young man who really wanted to sleep in on Sunday morning. His mother called up the stairs to remind him it was time to go to church. "I'm not going today!" he groaned as he turned over.

"Give me three good reasons," his mother said with a sigh.

"No problem," he said. "First, they don't like me over there. Second, no one cares about me anyway. Third, they won't even notice whether I'm there or not! And I'll bet you can't give me three good reasons to go!"

"Absolutely," Mom replied. "First, you are 30 years old and you shouldn't need your mom to tell you. Second, you live in my house and I say so. And third, you are the pastor!"

I haven't had it that bad, but I sure wanted to leave. Staying through pain or irritation or frustration has always been the best decision. I sometimes encounter people who don't care for me, and running away sounds appealing, but staying has a much stronger impact. In addition, people who attend church regularly, more often than just Sundays, have the privilege of watching their children come to love being a part of the true Bride of Christ.

With this come the spiritual disciplines of prayer and Bible reading. It is hard to find the time in today's busy families, but use every opportunity you can. "Families that pray together, stay together," may be more than just a slogan. As always, it's a matter of spiritual saturation.

Create Traditions

This may sound a little odd to be in a must-do list for the family, but it seems that families that create traditions also create stronger bonds. Everyone's family traditions differ, and I would certainly not suggest that the family traditions that we have are to be the same ones for your family. The issue is that families need to find things to do together, to hang out, to connect and stay connected. It will be well worth the time and effort.

What I mean by family traditions can be anything as simple as making s'mores every Sunday night during the summer, to vacations at a favorite spot, to some special family meal or activity. There is a

Some Important Must Do's For the Heart

long list of possibilities. You can cook that family meal together. You can have a "pick a dessert" night. You can do a family weekend, where each member chooses an activity. If you are into games, you can have a board game night. Our family chose several things to keep us close. For instance, we worked hard at getting away somewhere every year. It was fun to see how God would provide, but in the end, we found out that the beach was one of our family favorites. It gave us much time to just hang out together as a family. We chose not to allow our kids to bring friends, because we really coveted our time as a family and did not want to share that. We also began a number of Christmas traditions, which, with my wife's love of giving, often cost me dearly; however, those will be special memories that our kids will have forever. In addition, we often put family nights on our calendars. With everything so busy in our lives, we found out that if we did not schedule it, then someone else would steal the calendar. If we had a family night planned and someone invited us to an event, we could clearly say that we already have a commitment. Broken promises do not bode well with children, and nor should they.

Sunday afternoons were also very special. Even after preaching two times that morning, I would put the kids in the car and we would go somewhere. Often just to get a treat and play at a park. They loved when I played tag with them, because they always tricked me and I could never win. Wrestling was a family favorite as well. They loved to pile on Dad as he lay helpless on the floor. You should see some of the videos! That brings me to the next step of those family traditions: be sure to take photos or videos. You will never get those years back without at least some kind of visual reminder. We still pull out the videos and watch them. Of course I spend more time crying that those years have gone by way too fast, but they are our treasures until eternity. As a matter of fact I believe that our pictures and videos are more valuable to us than any other part of our house.

Some parents also learn to cook special foods for their kids. I still remember the two cakes my mom baked every Christmas and that my dad always cooked Christmas morning breakfast (the only morning Mom even allowed Dad into the kitchen). I can still smell the bacon! I have learned the specialty of chocolate milkshakes. Even today, if the kids are at home some evening, the request inevitably appears, "Dad, can you make us a milkshake?" If the ingredients are in our house, it is going to happen.

I Heart Parenting

Now I have not explained these ideas to you to boast of my Dad of the Year award. I can tell you that I have made many mistakes as a dad, and wished I could change them. What I have tried to show is the importance of having family traditions. It will be well worth the time.

When the nest is empty, you will have many days to finish projects, paint and draw, play golf, or whatever else you feel you must do. But you will never get their childhood years back. Don't cheat your children out of those great years and don't rush them forward. They will be gone fast enough, and there will come a time that your silent house will only contain echoes of the past. Parents who long for the day they will be empty nesters have lost the true joy of what it means to be a parent. I have loved every year of parenting, and only wish that there were more to come. I am sure I will enjoy my grandchildren, but my four children have come directly from me and the woman I love. There will never be another child like my four, and I miss their growing years so much. This past Christmas, when we opened gifts and talked of the Luke 2 account, it was just different that one was married and out of the house. Before long, all of them will be out of the house, and I will sit down one day over the Christmas break and watch a video of years past and cry over the fond memories the videos bring. Parents, redeem every moment of every day and create many traditions of family joy. It brings your children's hearts closer to you and toward God.

Be Consistent

As I've said before, if there is one thing children can spot, it is a hypocrite. When parents say one thing and expect their children to behave a certain way, while all the while they are doing the exact opposite, the children recognize the hypocrisy. To them, there is nothing more frustrating than seeing their parents act one way before the church and be different at home. Children need and must see consistency in their parents. True, a lack of consistency is no excuse for their rebellion. They must own their sin, but nevertheless, I have noticed over the years the many children who rebel often come from homes where parents are hypocrites.

Take, for example, the matter of respect. Parents often teach their children to respect their elders, which is commendable. But then they talk about those same adults disrespectfully. They complain about teachers, coaches, pastors, etc. at home. The children hear that and begin disrespecting that person. The attitude that should say, "I respect and obey you because you are in authority over me," now says, "Why should you tell me what to do or how to do it?" A recent situation illustrates this point: a group of girls had a young coach for their team. The parents were complaining because the coach was young. Evidently, they complained at home a lot, because after about two weeks, the girls, who had up to that point been respectful listeners, became a huge discipline problem. They didn't feel they needed to listen to the coach because their parents didn't respect her. Sadly, the parents then complained that the coach had no control over her team, when they were the cause of the problem!

Your most consistent behavior will show up in your children. I often hear parents say things like, "I don't know where my child picked up that attitude! We don't act like this at home." While there are always exceptions, parents need to stop blaming their kid's behavior on other families. I cannot think of one bad habit, sin, or behavior that my children picked up from somewhere other than their own heart, the devil, or our family as a whole. Again, I am sure that if little Johnnie plays next door with little Billie and Billie has a foul mouth, little Johnnie may bring some of that home. But the family's reaction to those bad words will say a lot about whether the language continues! The attitudes, behavior, and other long-lasting concerns are those that come from within, either the heart or the home. Stop blame-shifting and clean up at home first, and then move on from there. And for the sake of your children and the kingdom, talk the talk and walk the walk. Be consistent both at home and away.

Give Them a Correct View of Authority

One of the iconic bumper stickers of the liberal world agenda today might very well be the one that says "Question Authority." I am not suggesting that all authority is correct and fair in all situations and submission is the only option. Nevertheless, the bumper sticker's message sets a standard that the first response is to question the authority, and then if we approve of it or agree, we follow or submit. That is simply not the biblical view. What I do see in Scripture is clear teaching that when you are under authority, you are not to question it, but to do what you are told to do. Obedience ought to be a correct attitude. There is no room for grumbling and complaining and whining about the situation. Just do what you are told to do (unless it clearly violates God's Word).

I suspect that most parents would love it if their child would comprehend this concept and do what they were told to do with a right attitude. Yet so many children behave exactly the opposite way! How can a parent get their child to respond in obedience? Well, first it begins with the parent understanding their position of being under authority. And I can tell you as a pastor, there are very few adults who truly understand authority.

Many of today's parents and grandparents are those who came out of one of the greatest eras of questioning authority in the history of our country. These parents were in college, burning buildings, bras, and anything that had to do with support or authority. While they were out finding themselves, they were also trashing the establishment. These folks from the 60–70's eventually went on to become parents and now grandparents. They helped develop a generation that had little or no respect for authority. And now some of their offspring have bumper stickers to prove it. One man put it this way: "When my kids were young, I taught them to question authority. When they got older, they questioned mine."

This poison of anti-authority runs throughout a generation that has very little respect for any authority. As a child, I learned to call every adult by Mr. or a Mrs., and to say "Yes, Ma,am" and "Yes Sir." Often an adult would ask me not to call him or her by that because it sounded old, but it was spoken out of respect for authority, not age. There was one particularly old man in our community who probably had something resembling Alzheimer's disease. Once I made fun of him, but I was instantly rebuked by my parents. My mom and dad expected me to respect my elders, no matter what condition they were in. The lesson I learned on that day has remained with me. Even today, I still call some of my former professors by their full, titled name. How do we draw this generation back to a mindset of biblical authority?

Again, as with so many other issues, it begins in the home. Children who grow up in homes where authority is modeled and taught will be more responsive in the areas of authority than those who do not. Although it is painful to admit, the children of our generation are struggling with authority because they see their parents model a lack of respect for authority. They are struggling to respond to authority when they are seeing it differently with Mom and Dad. So how should the parents model this in the home? First and foremost is their submission to God. Kids should be well aware of what Scripture says about church, prayer, Bible reading, tithing, serving, and all the principles that are also pertinent today. Most kids can give a fairly accurate report on their parents' spiritual lives. They know what the Bible says about these things and they know whether their parents are living it. Parents who are rebellious toward God's authority produce children who are rebellious to God's authority. You cannot expect them to live what you are not willing to model. If you want your children to walk with God, then, dear parent, it begins with you. Get serious about your salvation and model it in such a way that your children emulate your walk. Paul asked his followers to follow him as he followed Christ. That ought to be the motto of every parent.

Another area of submission is the church. Be under the authority of the leadership of your church. I can promise you that if you have roasted preacher every Sunday afternoon for dinner, your children are going to walk away from the church. You are instilling rebellion to authority in your home. I grew up in a home that greatly respected the pastors and the church. In all my early years, I never once heard my parents speak negatively about the church. As a matter of fact, the pastors were often in our home, especially for important family occasions. They were as much a part of us as our family itself. When God called me to pastor, I had this view in back of my mind. That foundation laid by my parents was part of what God used to soften my heart to His leading. Yet I wonder how many pastors are not in the pulpit today because of parents?

The next area of focus is between husbands and wives. What a volatile subject! The home is such a place of importance, and if this area is not right, it will cause problems that are hard to repair later. I remember seeing a comic where the mailman was bringing several large bags of mail to the pastor's house. The caption read something like: "I see you were preaching on wives submitting to husbands again." Well, the mailman might just be delivering some of that mail to me after this section, but whether we like it or not, it is in the Scripture: "Wives, submit to your husbands, as unto the Lord" (Eph 5:22). The problem for us is: what exactly does it mean?

It might be easier at the first to state what it does not mean. It does not mean that men are dictators and women have no rights. It does not mean that men are to drag their wives around by the hair, or that women are to live their lives in the kitchen. It does not mean that women have no say. A very familiar part of the wedding ceremony is called the lighting of the unity candle. It is a moving component where the mothers of the bride and groom go up to the front and light each a candle on the outside of a larger centerpiece candle at the beginning of the service. The idea is that they are symbolically lighting a candle to represent the beginning of the lives of the bride and groom. Then at some time during the wedding ceremony, the bride and groom retrieve their respective candles and together help light the large center candle. Both the bride and the groom blow out their candle as a symbol of the two becoming one. Now the picture itself is very striking, but in actuality, you don't stop existing as an individual when you are married. I believe it would be best to just bring the two candles together to help make a bigger light, and one light. But the individual candle ought to still exist. Women are as important in the marriage just as the men. Yet the truth is still clear; Christ was subject to the Father, and women ought to be subject to their husbands. Now what exactly does that look like?

While we do not have time to do an in-depth study on the passage, here is how I believe this ought to be played out in the home. At no time should Mom and Dad argue in front of the kids. At no time should Mom or Dad go behind their mate's back and undermine the other person's authority. You may believe you are helping the child, but undermining your mate only builds rebellion toward authority. You may not realize that the child will learn to rebel against you as well. You think you are winning them over, but it is just the opposite. You are creating rebellion, and you will personally see the effects of that rebellion. Moms and dads need to discuss their disagreements in private, and when the discussion is over, they need to come out together on the issue. There ought to be equal discussion and equal respect and equal thought put into the matter. Just because one thinks something, does not make it right. But the problem occurs when Mom and Dad cannot agree on an issue.

There are several options here. First, there might be a need to get outside advice/counsel as from your pastor, especially if the matter is serious. Another option is for one side to just let it go. We have a saying

Some Important Must Do's For the Heart

in our home "LIG," meaning "Let it go." Some things just are not worth the fight. If there's a decision to be made, pray about it! A couple that grabs each other's hands and calls out to God is taking a vital step in the decision-making process. It is also important to be sensitive to the mate who may have a better view of the situation. Suppose that the issue surrounds your daughter. Who might be better to deal with a girl issue than the mom? I am not saying moms are always right on daughters and dads are always right on sons, but it is worth examining as a general rule. It is also important to examine whom the decision affects the most. Suppose the issue involves driving the child to activities that might take place nightly or often. Which parent is going to have to handle most of that responsibility? Decisions like that must be made with sensitivity toward the parent who will carry the greater load.

We could add more in this discussion, but let's get to the main point that often causes the most difficult problems in the process. When the dust settles and the problem has been given a fair and balanced approach, the final response must come from Dad. How that exactly is fleshed out will differ for each home, but I can assure you that if this is not properly managed in your home, your children may very well develop a rebellious heart.

Some other areas of submission to authority include the government, police, military, elected officials, and employers. Parents who model proper understanding of authority are more likely to produce children who respond well to these authorities. I am concerned that children who grow up in homes that do not respect those in authority are simply going to parrot that view. More is caught than taught.

One final thought about authority that needs to be added here. If the child lives at home or is being financed in some way by the parents, then there is no question that they are under your authority. I hear children say all the time, "I am 18 and I can do whatever I want." It is like the kid who is tired of being under his parents' authority so he joins the Marines where someone else can control him! There is no magic number of when you are no longer under authority. The only hint in Scripture that I find is when you leave father and mother and cleave to your wife. That is symbolically pictured when the dad hands his daughter over to her future husband at the altar and before a pastor and before God. Until that "handing off," the child is under the parents' authority. Now I realize that some children marry much later in life and how late do we take that thought. That will have to be worked out in every family, but the overall thought is under authority until the wedding day. That includes also college. I remember one of my daughters calling me from college and asking about an ear piercing. She was at the mall with college friends, and they were getting extra piercings and she wanted to do so. She called me and asked my advice and permission. She said her friends told her that she was on her own and did not need to do so, but we had taught her differently. She commented that her friends all had told her that when she was dropped off at college, she was on her own. Now I find that very fascinating. I was paying for her college degree, insurance, phone, and all the other incidentals, but her friends' mindset was that she could do what she wanted. How does that work? And I strongly encourage parents to remember that while the child lives under your roof (including college years), you are the parents and they are under your authority. Again, how that exactly is fleshed out is up to each family, but stop trying to be their friend and be their parent.

Bless Them without Spoiling Them

There is nothing wrong with positive and Christ-centered affirmation. Scripture says in numerous places how much God loves us, cares for us, provides for us, and affirms us. We are in Christ and blessed because of that. But parents who want to bless and affirm through giving things to their kids can be running pretty strong risk of spoiling them. God does not just indiscriminately give to us, nor should we give that way to our children. Giving is acceptable, but it needs to be in the confines of balance and appropriateness. I have seen very young children walking through the mall with their own cell phone. Now there might come a time for a child to need a phone, but for the most part, the cell phone is a luxury and a status symbol.

Children who are given things with no particular connection to reason or logic grow up believing the world owes them a living. They continue to expect the Publisher's Clearing House to come through for them, or feel that the lottery officials will call them any day. They will also learn to expect Mom and Dad to be ready to give them anything they want. They don't learn to appreciate what they have, and instead develop a mindset of continually wanting more. By contrast, children who learn that they must earn the things they want, find that life is about that same mindset. A boss is not going to give them promotions and raises just because they work for him. Life is not that way. Our goal is to help prepare our children for the real world, not some imagined world that has fairy godmothers and parents who don't know when to say "no."

There might be a thin line between blessing them and spoiling them. Most parents want to give to their children what they did not have as a child. There is some room to do so, but what we have observed is that when these children marry, they attempt to have everything their parents have, not understanding that it took their parents an entire life to accumulate those things. So, the child operates with that mindset, often becoming financially strapped to a home, car payment, and in some cases, credit card debt (God forbid). They need to see their parents working for things, and they need to understand that deferred gratification is normal.

The best way to discern the correct response to your child's desires is to distinguish between a want and a need. Without question this is a difficult discernment, but it must be made with care and prayer. If a child *needs* something, parents should do all that they can do to provide for that need. That is part of our role as parents. Of course, if you ask the child, those sneakers for $300 are a need, as compared to the ones for $40. There may be a time to buy the more expensive ones, but be cautious about setting precedents and standards that will be hard to meet throughout the life of a child. I often go to games and watch friends or family members play in the little tots' leagues in our area. I am greatly amused when I see six-year-olds come out with shoes more expensive than the ones I wear going to church! The same kid will have a $2 drink and designer sweat bands. If an athlete swears by a certain kind of undergarment, you can be sure it will be on most kids in sports. Will the extra $260 truly help the child shoot, dribble, or defend better? Do you really think so? Blessing comes through positive affirmation, while spoiling comes about by giving that which is unnecessary and unfruitful to a child. Beware of creating an attitude of insatiable materialism!

Give Them a Normal Home

While we can't give them every *thing* they want, we can strive to give them what is most important: a normal home. Of course, the question of what "normal" looks like is hotly debated today. Years ago, that was a much easier discussion. Dad went to work, Mom stayed home, and the family stayed together, prayed together, and were a positive addition to society. Today, there are many different views as to what a normal home may entail. Nevertheless, there are a few components that should be included in every normal home.

It ought to be a home that is safe for the family, including safety from internal and external harm. It is a place where the child can sleep at night free of fears and dangers. It may mean that you have to regularly look under the bed and in the closet for the boogey man, but that's a parent's job. A few minutes of dispelling fears will go a long way for a worry-free rest for all. And by the way, avoid having little Junior regularly sleep with you. A couple's bed is exactly what it is—room for Mom and Dad. Now there may be a few storms that require this privilege, but if Junior is regularly coming in for a night at the parents' expense, something must be done. For example, we used to have on Friday nights where all our children slept in our room. They brought in sleeping bags and pillows and blankets and it was a night to remember. Wow do I ever miss those times! On the rest of the days, they stayed in their own rooms.

There should be a lot of laughter in the home, as well. I heard one great man near the end of his life say that if there was one thing he would do more often if he had his life to live over, he would laugh more. Too many parents take their role too seriously. Parenting is serious (as I've explained frequently throughout this book), but we need to learn to laugh at ourselves and with each other. As we look back, there are many times when we wish he had just laughed instead of lowering the boom. Face it—we do stupid things, and stupid things are funny. Just watch stupid videos on YouTube. Laughter in a home is a non-negotiable. There is too much pain and sorrow in the real world. We don't need to add any more pain to the overall picture. I believe there were too many times where I took a situation far more seriously than necessary. But every once in a while, I got the humor right. One such episode was when our twins were still in diapers. They had a tendency to literally destroy their bedroom during this time. We would come in to the room after the "quiet" hour was over and discover all the clothes out of the dresser, the closet pulled out and every sheet and blanket all over the place. I am not sure exactly what they thought they were doing. On one occasion, my wife went up to get the girls up from their nap and I heard a loud scream from her as she entered. She then called to me to come up and bring the camera. It was going to be a memory in the making. I came up to see the normal mess, but no children were around. The only logical place was under the bed for them, and as we peeked under, two naked rear ends were staring at us. Yes, they had taken their diapers off. Now keep in mind, there is a reason for the diaper to be on the child—namely, poop control. Not this time. The ingredients that ought to have stayed in the diaper were used as finger paint for the entire room. It was going to take hours to straighten and clean up. We looked at each other and just began laughing. Those cute butts were not going to be disciplined on this day, but we sure have the video to enjoy for years to come, and hopefully embarrass them at the right time. Bottoms up and laugh a little more. The joy of parenting far exceeds the pains if you choose to rejoice in the Lord always.

A normal home ought to be also a home where the child can truly blossom. Give them every reasonable opportunity to become all that God intended for them to be. That will require you to know the mind of Christ and have the heart of God for your children. These children need parents who will love them, exhort them, challenge them, but also know them. Even if both parents are doctors, that doesn't mean the child will be a doctor. A normal home is a balanced home and little Johnnie may need piano lessons. God may give you an athlete just to mix things up. Remember that our Lord is a truly amazing God and He loves to do that which we would never think of doing. Keep in mind that it is hard to produce normal kids when in fact most parents are anything but normal! Your home should give children the right and privilege to make mistakes. Kids are not perfect and they are going to mess up. Knowing when to step in and when to allow them to make mistakes is a difficult challenge. Keep close to God and He will show you. Remember that He loves those children more than you do. Learn from the Master Father and give them the normal home He desires for them.

Give Them a Home with Structure, Boundaries, and Discipline

Before we leave this section, I want to talk about three parts of parenting that I have intentionally lumped together. Children need all three from their parents, and the more you can incorporate them into the home, the more balanced and focused the home will be.

Believe it or not, children do better with structure: structure in the bed time, meal time, and play time. The more structure you can give them the better, specifically structure with meaning and purpose. Aimless structure has no purpose, and structure to just have structure makes no sense. Use the structure to help shape your children. Have structured mealtimes and bedtimes when they are young. Children who have certain issues like ADHD may need a very strict structure through all their growing up years in order to get a handle on the issue. Other children may be able to add spontaneity once in a while, so long as it is added within an overall framework. Have structure and have boundaries, both for what they can and cannot do.

I am not going to make discipline a major component of this book. Scripture is clear: spare the rod and spoil the child (Proverbs 13:24). Again, every family is going to have to flesh the meaning out on its own. The exact specifics of discipline, I believe, are negotiable. What is not negotiable is the issue of discipline. Discipline is a must and each family must spend careful time in determining the best options for their children. What may work for one child may not even work for another child. Some children need only a stern look to correct them. Others won't even waver and need other measures. Whatever type of discipline works well, there are a few absolutes that parents must follow:

1. Don't ever discipline in anger.
2. Be consistent.
3. Follow through with what you say you are going to do.
4. Don't apply the counting system because it only teaches delayed obedience.
5. Agree to the exact details of the discipline.
6. Be sure to let the child know why they are being disciplined.

Disciplining correctly will allow the parent to ensure that even if the child isn't happy, they will understand the lesson and, hopefully, learn from it!

To Wrap it Up

Parenting is a full-time work that must not be taken lightly. As you seek the Lord's wisdom, He will help you shape the hearts of your children for eternal values. Look for areas where you may be weak or failing, and ask God to help you strengthen those. Pray for guidance in areas where His will seems cloudy. And remember that He will guard you as you seek to guard and guide your children!

Finally, I believe we need to see how important it is to give our children Jesus. We do so by having a personal relationship with Jesus first and foremost. You truly can't give something away that you do not have yourself. Then do all you can to live for Jesus. Your light needs to shine before men (Matt 5:16), but also before family. Don't be a Christian at church and a non-Christian at home. Your faith ought to be plainly visible. And as you give to them Jesus with your life, do all you can to saturate them with Jesus 24/7. The best place to start changing the world is at home.

14

FAQs About the Heart of Parenting

JUST AS NOT ALL children fit into a specific parenting mold, all the issues surrounding parenting don't fit neatly into specific chapter headings. Therefore, I have created a chapter that really is a conglomeration of issues, questions, and difficulties that parents face. I don't expect that this will cover all possibilities, but I am hoping these will help with some of the common questions and offer discussion possibilities for you and your spouse.

Where Do Grandparents Fit In?

Grandparents play an important role in the home structure. Unfortunately, many grandparents are not included into the extended family as they should be, either by choice or by exclusion. This deprives the children of many benefits.

Growing up near my maternal grandparents (my paternal ones were deceased) was clearly one of the greatest blessings of my childhood. In many ways, my Pop was my hero and quite possibly my best friend. I did more with him than probably any other person during critical years of my development. I was named after him, which might have given us a bond, but we became kindred spirits. Parents need to be intentional in getting grandparents actively involved in their grandchildren's lives, assuming of course that there is no negative reason for keeping them away from each other. There are a number of ways to involve them:

1. Get the grandparents involved in their grandchildren's lives. Very often grandparents are retired and have much extra time to invest. Be creative and go after this opportunity.

FAQs About the Heart of Parenting

2. Avoid letting the grandparents meddle. They are to be a blessing, not a curse.

3. Give them specific prayer requests to be praying for your children.

4. Invite them to as many special occasions as possible, especially if they don't know the Lord. Having them at the baptism, plays and performances, etc., can be a great means to reach their hearts.

5. Understand that grandparents love to spoil grandchildren. Let them do so, within reason. It is one of the few joys getting older affords them.

6. Understand that they are not as young as they used to be. Don't put so much on them, such as full-time day care over your kids, unless they are willing and able. They did not retire to raise your children.

7. Teach your children to respect their grandparents. This is often very hard, especially if you believe that they do not deserve it. But remember, you will be the grandparents one day.

Your parents are not going to live forever. They will likely pass away during the lifetime of your family. You don't want to have regrets, and you don't want your children to miss out here. It might take some steps of humility, but the children will be the blessed for your sacrifice.

What About Clothing?

There might not be a more difficult area for parents than the issue of clothing. Children have always pushed the envelope on the clothing styles, and parents often find themselves on the losing end. It typically has been easier to just cave in and allow the child to wear whatever than to fight over the outfit. That also goes with piercings, tattoos, and whatever other fad will be around by the time this book is finished. Please remember—our bodies are not our own. We have been bought with a price (meaning all of us), and we belong to God. God needs to permit what we do with the body. If I borrowed your car, would you be happy if I put bumper stickers all over it? You would argue, rightly, that the car was not mine. We shouldn't feel any differently when we contemplate these bodies that are "on loan" to us from the Savior!

Clothing, especially for girls, is so discouraging for most parents. Going to the mall to buy stylish, yet modest clothing is becoming an increasingly difficult challenge. I love that new group called "Modest is Hottest." I believe they have their own website and tee shirts. Girls need to understand that being modest is not really an option. But if parents leave the clothing up to their children, many will chose the popular styles and ignore the modesty aspect.

I am not going to set up some arbitrary standard that is basically impossible to measure: skirts need to be so long, pants cannot be this tight, tops cannot be that low, and clothes cannot be this way is a battle that will not work. Every family must take the time to determine the appropriate style, standard, and measurement of clothing. Modesty is not an option, and if the clothing is revealing, it is inappropriate. Bathing suits are also very troublesome areas, but parents need to take time to discover proper clothing and solutions.

Parents, please convey this to your girls: boys are stimulated by the visual. Seeing flesh causes them to think thoughts that are sometimes difficult for them. Don't feed their fleshly desires. Perfumes can also be distracting, so guard against an overabundance of that as well. Of course, you don't want to look ratty and you really don't want to smell bad, but one can be fashionable without being revealing. And just as boys must get their thoughts under control, girls must not do things to cause them to stumble. Watch how you bend over with the style of tops today. Watch how you cross your legs with the tightness of skirts or dresses. Watch how tight-fitting clothing may reveal a lot of your body to those who struggle. If you don't watch your clothing carefully, boys will. Each person sins because of their own heart, but we must not do anything to cause our brother to sin. There is blame to go around. It would not hurt a girl to talk with their dad about the dangers in this area with Mom present at the discussion.

What if My Child Wants to Date?

Many parents make a mistake by saying that since they survived the dating scene, they are sure that their children will survive it as well. Let me make one point clear: teens today have seen more bed scenes than you saw before you were married. Between the videos, the movies, the internet, and so many other sources with sexual content, their drives are much stronger than those their parents dealt with as teens. Sure, the sexual drive was there, but the stimuli that foster the drive were nowhere near as accessible. Teens today are saturated with sexual information and know more about this area than many of our generation did until they were married. We are kidding ourselves if we believe that this is harmless information. In our public schools today, teens can obtain birth control items without parental knowledge or consent. You had better not take the dating scene lightly! Some parents prefer courtship over dating. I would suggest you do some research into that area and make an informed decision. I personally think there is much good in the courtship suggestion. But since many choose the dating route, let me add a few thoughts for guidance:

1. Never allow your child to go on single dates. There is simply no reason for two teens to go off for a night without supervision.

2. Never allow your "daters" time alone, either in the basement or car or wherever.

3. Make sure you get to know the person before they are given the permission to date your child. Do you know the family, the person, the past, or whatever?

4. Do not allow any dating before 16 at a minimum. I know that sounds strong, but too many children are hurt at an early age and your calling, remember, is to protect that heart. Early crushes can have long-term effects.

5. Give your 16-year-old girl a purity ring or necklace of some sort. We took our girls out for a formal dinner and discussed purity with them when they turned 16. We then gave them a ring and explained that it was a symbol of keeping themselves pure for their mate. At no time were they to ever violate this commitment between us and them. If they did so, they were to return the ring. You can do something similar for boys—give them something to carry in their wallet.

6. Just because they have the ring, do not give them scenarios where the compromise may happen. Do not allow them alone time in the house by themselves. Parents—stupidity is no excuse here. Children are curious about sex and will test the waters; even the best of kids will do so if given too much leeway.

I Heart Parenting

7. When and how much you explain sex to your children is under great debate. It is like the little girl who came up and asked her Mom "what is sex?" The mom, thinking that her child was ready, gave her the full story. Dumb decision. After the whole story, the little girl asked her mom, "But which box should I check? The one with the M or the one with the F?" Be sure they are ready for the full story. I believe children should learn about sex from Mom or Dad, preferably Mom for the girls and Dad for the boys. If you don't, they will learn from someone else, and what they learn may not be godly.

Dating is a tough question, and parents have come up with all kinds of different ways to protect their children. I came across Daddy's Ten Rules of Dating and thought you might enjoy some of these "regulations":

Daddy's Ten Rules of Dating

Rule One:

If you pull into my driveway and honk, you'd better be delivering a package, because you're sure not picking anything up.

Rule Two:

You do not touch my daughter in front of me. You may glance at her, so long as you do not peer at anything below her neck. If you cannot keep your eyes or hands off of my daughter's body, I will remove them.

Rule Three:

I am aware that it is considered fashionable for boys of your age to wear their trousers so loosely that they appear to be falling off their hips. Please don't take this as an insult, but you and all of your friends are complete idiots. Still, I want to be fair and open minded about this issue, so I propose this compromise: You may come to the door with your underwear showing and your pants ten sizes too big, and I will not object. However, in order to ensure that your clothes do not, in fact, come off during the course of your date with my daughter, I will take my electric nail gun and fasten your trousers securely in place to your waist.

FAQs About the Heart of Parenting

Rule Four:
> I'm sure you've been told that in today's world, sex without utilizing a "barrier method" of some kind can kill you. Let me elaborate: when it comes to sex, I am the barrier, and I will kill you.

Rule Five:
> It is usually understood that in order for us to get to know each other, we should talk about sports, politics, and other issues of the day. Please do not do this. The only information I require from you is an indication of when you expect to have my daughter safely back at my house, and the only word I need from you on this subject is: "early."

Rule Six:
> I have no doubt you are a popular fellow, with many opportunities to date other girls. This is fine with me as long as it is okay with my daughter. Otherwise, once you have gone out with my little girl, you will continue to date no one but her until she is finished with you. If you make her cry, I will make you cry.

Rule Seven:
> As you stand in my front hallway, waiting for my daughter to appear, and more than an hour goes by, do not sigh and fidget. If you want to be on time for the movie, you should not be dating. My daughter is putting on her makeup, a process than can take longer than painting the Golden Gate Bridge. Instead of just standing there, why don't you do something useful, like changing the oil in my car?

Rule Eight:
> The following places are not appropriate for a date with my daughter: Places where there are beds, sofas, or anything softer than a wooden stool. Places where there is darkness. Places where there is dancing, holding hands, or happiness. Places where the ambient temperature is warm enough to induce my daughter to wear shorts, tank tops, midriff T-shirts, or anything other than overalls, a sweater, and a goose down parka zipped up to her throat. Movies with a strong romantic or sexual theme are to be avoided; movies which feature chain saws are okay. Hockey games are okay. Old folks homes are better.

I Heart Parenting

Rule Nine:
> Do not lie to me. I may appear to be a potbellied, balding, middle-aged, dimwitted has-been. But on issues relating to my daughter, I am the all-knowing, merciless god of your universe. If I ask you where you are going and with whom, you have one chance to tell me the truth, the whole truth and nothing but the truth. I have a shotgun, a shovel, and five acres behind the house. Do not trifle with me.

Rule Ten:
> Be afraid. Be very afraid. It takes very little for me to mistake the sound of your car in the driveway for a chopper coming in over a rice paddy near Hanoi. When my Agent Orange starts acting up, the voices in my head frequently tell me to clean the guns as I wait for you to bring my daughter home. As soon as you pull into the driveway you should exit the car with both hands in plain sight. Speak the perimeter password, announce in a clear voice that you have brought my daughter home safely and early, then return to your car; there is no need for you to come inside. The camouflaged face at the window is mine.

Ok, maybe the above information goes a little overboard (and I know it is slightly dated with the Vietnam War reference). It was really hyperbole driven, but you can see that this parent is in earnest! Hopefully the over-the-top challenge will cause some parents to take a closer look at the dating scene. Personally, I have seen very little good come out of that area. They cut their other friends off. They become consumed with their boyfriend/girlfriend and begin to live a world totally void of family and God. Parents begin to take the boyfriends/girlfriends everywhere as if they are part of the family. They see each other every day and every weekend. Parents, this is too much. Put a stop to their self-consumed world and teach them that this world is bigger than they are. And if their coming together as a dating couple is not impacting the Kingdom, then why let them do it? I would challenge families to take more caution in this area than what is typical, and do all you can to guard the heart of your child. They have all the necessary components to become parents, and if left alone, they just might do so. Is it worth the risk? You decide, but remember that you are responsible to be the guardians of your children.

How Do I Cut the Apron Strings?

Letting go is never an easy discussion. Today it seems that more and more children are returning home after college for some years. After four years of college with less parental oversight, they are now home and the boundaries are not as clear. What principles help transition your kids from childhood to adulthood?

We must examine the whole question of adulthood first. When does a child become an adult? That is not an easy discussion. I have met some very mature 16-year-olds, and some very immature 25-year-olds. Each child must be evaluated separately. I don't personally believe that we want to land on a certain age for adulthood. Far too many children think that when they graduate from high school, that they are now an adult. If they can fight in a war or go to college or begin a career or get married, then surely they are an adult. However, I don't see a light switch go on at 18. Much of the outcome of debate will rest on the goals and directions of the parents. Logically, whoever is paying the bills has the authority. The only time I see a transfer in Scripture is on the wedding day. You can discuss this further as a family, but marriage seems to be the proper time to cut the apron springs and let little Janie fly.

Also, I believe there are steps to letting go. Begin to give young teens responsibility so that they start to prepare to deal with this world "on their own." As they learn to take on more and more responsibility and respond well to those responsibilities, then more liberties can be given. For example, if the child is to be home from an event by a certain time and they don't make curfew, then there ought to be some caution about the next privilege. If a child flunks out of college, maybe they need to begin paying for college on their own? If they total a car or lose their cell phone, maybe they do without for a while. Cutting the apron strings needs to be done over time. You are to be raising that child towards that goal. But you need to make sure you have properly prepared them to be in the world and not of the world. All that you do when they are under your roof is to prepare their hearts to hear from God and to obey His leading. While they are under your roof, they are getting that lead from the parents. On their own, they will need to discover it themselves. If you have trained them well, they will know how to walk with God.

What if I Have a Divided Home?

A divided home is one where only one parent is a believer, the parents are not on the same page, or a separation/divorce has occurred. These situations make it very difficult for the one who is trying to do the correct things in parenting. Often one mate will undermine the other's authority, especially if it relates to the spiritual. But just because something is difficult does not make the situation impossible. A people of faith must never lose faith in a God who is able to do amazing things for His glory.

First Corinthians 7:14 gives a picture very similar to what the above situations entail. Paul states the believer that is in the marriage has a sanctifying effect on the entire family. His point is that God will bless the believer in such a way that the blessing will overflow to those that are not. Greater is He that is in you and in the home than he that is in the opposition who may also live in the home or be wherever your kids are. Even if you have been losing most of the battles and the custody has gone against you, take heart. God loves those children more than you ever will. He loved them so much that He sent His Son to die for them. He even warns about hurting children and the consequences that go with it. God wants to bless the family because of the believers in the family. Even if there is only one believer, you all make up the majority, because God and you are always larger than whoever may try to be on the other side. You need a fresh view of faith and hope and belief in the God who loves to do that which no one could even suspect. But as you exercise your faith, here are a few hints to help along the way.

Make this a serious matter of prayer. You need God's hand of guidance because you truly are in a difficult situation. You need to speak His Words and walk the walk that He has laid out for you. There is a time to speak and time to be quiet. There is a time to confront and a time to walk away. There is a time to stay and there is a time to run. Only God can tell you the best in each case, and only God can know what is best. Counsel can be helpful, but ultimately this must be fleshed out on your knees.

Do all you can to avoid making the situation worse than it is. Avoid pushing your mate's buttons. You know what I mean. If your mate hates to see you reading your Bible, read it while he is not around. I am not saying that you cave into every whim of your mate, but avoid antagonizing. Now if he would say that he does not want you to ever read your Bible, then you must obey God rather than man. I do not believe you should ever disobey God to save your marriage. God always comes first, and if you give into a human's efforts to dissuade you from God, then you are putting someone ahead of God. God hates divorce, but He expects you to always put Him first and leave the consequences to Him.

Finally, take the right time to discuss differences and how to handle them. Very few, even if they are unbelievers, enjoy conflict. No one wants a home divided, and it might be that you were saved after marriage and are now a different person than your spouse married. You need to be sensitive to the fact that he or she did not sign up to be married to a Christian. So, be patient and utilize the right time to discuss differences. The best way to handle any family issue is to be on the same page. Finding common ground is helpful to keep the communications lines open and less stressful. Begin the discussion with what is working, and slowly go to the more difficult. Take time and effort and bathe with prayer. Remember that God is on your side, but He does not bless ignorance or stupidity that can be avoided. Look for His leading and follow it.

What if My Child is Rebellious and Nothing is Working?

One of the most difficult times for a parent is when they are already in the heat of the battle. It is one thing to deal with a two-year-old; you can pick him up and hold him to make him listen to you, but try that on a 200-pound 16-year-old! What is a parent to do when the child is already behaving rebelliously?

As always, the first necessity is to stay on your knees. Spiritual warfare must not be taken lightly, and this is spiritual warfare. Satan has an advantage, and we need to ask the Father to remove the enemy from the territory; Satan has no right to interfere. "The effective, fervent prayer of a righteous man avails much" (James 5:16, NKJV). Don't discount prayer. God loves to hear the prayers of a desperate child, just as any parent would respond to the cries of their children.

Deal with the rebellion directly and head on. Too many families avoid talking about the obvious in hopes that it will go away, or no one

I Heart Parenting

is going to get hurt. Let me be blunt: I doubt it is going away on its own, and people are going to get hurt. Rebellion is as the sin of witchcraft, and when the enemy gets a stronghold, he will not let go without a fight. Try to figure out why your child is behaving the way that he or she is. Try to get close to your child so you can discover what lies underneath. Spend time with your child to encourage confidence. You are your children's first line of defense and they need you, whether they understand that or not. Be sure to be their parent and not a friend. They need their mom or dad especially when rebellion has taken root. They probably would not say that, but it is true. Children need boundaries and parents need to set them in place. Don't give them the license to gravitate toward sinful behavior.

Get outside help. It is hard to see what the problem is or what is missing while you in the midst of the storm. I would begin with your pastor or elder who has been placed over your family for spiritual protection and guidance. It would be best if both parents go and visit the pastor first, and then begin a plan of guidance. Your pastor will know the best steps to take, especially if you are attending a Christ-centered church with a Christ-centered pastor. Don't let your pride keep you from coming clean with all the information to help the assessment. Hiding information due to embarrassment does not help in the process. By the way, parents are very gullible to think that they are hiding their children's behavior. Kids talk and post information on their favorite social media sites all the time; their friends will know what's going on a lot better than their parents do! I remember on one occasion that our youth leaders found some pictures a girl had posted on Facebook while in her freshman year of college. When we tried to inform the parents, they were more upset about the fact that people knew about it and obviously were talking about it than about what their child was doing. It was very sad. But I share this story with you to help you realize that there is a good chance what you think you know in secret is already being reported from the housetops. Another example is when a family finds out their child is promiscuous. Please don't be offended by what I am about to say, but promiscuous girls dress provocatively. You are fooling yourself if you believe differently. You will not shock your pastor by telling him you think your daughter is sexually active. Get help soon, for the difficulty is only going to increase. If your pastor cannot help for whatever reason, find a godly set of parents that you greatly admire and go and talk with them. Leave your pride at home, humble yourself, and cry out for help. Your children are worth the fight.

There are No Guarantees in Parenting

I greatly wish I could give you a 12-step program that guarantees a product that is God-fearing and God-centered. Scripture doesn't give such guarantees. There are those who like to quote verses such as, "Train up a child in the way he should go and when he is old he will not depart from it" (Pr 22:6). That's a great verse, but it does not say what many are attempting to claim from it. Yes I believe in training up the child, but the heart is desperately wicked and sinful (Jer 17:9). Don't let the fact that there are "no guarantees" stop you from doing what is right. The odds are greatly in your favor that you will produce a godly line if you raise your child to walk after God.

The principles and suggestions offered in this book have been proved and tried by many over the years and there has been great success and godly results. All throughout Scripture, the Lord has honored obedience to God-ordained actions and behavior. He sees our attempts to do what is right, although we fail often. He rewards our actions that are at least an effort to honor Him in all we do. God-centered parenting and going after the heart of the children truly lines up with Scriptural principles and God clearly takes notice of this parenting effort. So, although there are no guarantees, there are principles that certainly put the odds much more in your favor of raising a godly generation. Saturation and intentional parenting are all aimed at the heart of the child to bring them to a place where every child desires and wants to obey God. If the child's heart can be brought to this understanding, there are tremendous possibilities that your children will not be rebellious and will not bring heartache to the Lord or you. This kind of teaching is about as close to a guarantee that you will ever hear. Applying these principles may not be the perfect solution, but the results have and will speak for themselves. Even for some reason if the child still rebels, you will know before God that you have given your best at raising children in the fear of the Lord.

15

Parenting from a Mom's Perspective

Throughout this book, you've had a dad's perspective on parenting. It is worthwhile, however, to get a mom's view of these issues as well. Women often see things differently than men (no surprise there), so a mom's insights will be particularly valuable for the women reading this book. But men, don't skip this chapter—you may learn some things about parenting from a different standpoint!

BEING A MOM IS one of the most incredible blessings God has given to me this side of heaven. I was thrilled when my husband came up with the title of this book, because it truly describes how we view parenting. That does not mean it has been easy, nor does it mean we have done everything correctly. It does mean, though, that we have loved being parents and wish that everyone else cherished their God-given assignment. We know that it is not a simple task; in fact, we recognize that it is full of challenges and difficulties. If you are reading this book, that probably means you are looking for some type of encouragement as you parent. It is our hope and prayer that the message of this book does just that.

One chapter on being a mom—really? I could write an entire book, or teach a complete semester of Sunday school lessons on just being a mom. Scripture is filled with so much for us as moms, and goodness gracious, raising four daughters has given me plenty of personal illustrations! I've made mistakes and learned so much over the years, I could talk for hours. But, I've only got one chapter, so I will condense what is in my heart to share with you.

First, let me encourage you to view being a mom for what it really is. It is a blessing from God. "Children are a heritage from the Lord" (Ps

127:3). The Bible tells us that our children are a gift from God directly to us. While my child might have brown eyes and dimples and look just like me, I did not create her. I did not get the option to pick her out. If I did, I would have picked the exact four children He gave me! But I am merely making the point that God chooses which children we are given. Even in cases of adoption, we need to recognize God's sovereignty in allowing the adoption to come to fruition.

Recognizing that your child is a gift, personally chosen just for you, should direct your focus and perspective. Parenting truly is a God-given assignment. He allowed you to be a parent and He chose a specific bundle of DNA to be yours: a gift from heaven to your home. Sadly, there are women who would love to be called Mom, and for whatever reason, God has not chosen to bestow that blessing upon them. There are mothers who are in extreme circumstances, who are not able to care for and raise their children. You have yours right with you. That hand-picked, fearfully and wonderfully made gift belongs to you. God loves you so much that He chose to entrust you with one of his most beautiful creations—a child for whom Jesus died on the cross. Have you ever received a physical gift any more wonderful than that?

Next, you do not have to parent alone. We need to recognize that God is not some type of Santa who drops gifts off at your house and flies away in a sleigh. How you parent is very important to Him. He really has given you the tools that you need. They are called the Bible and the Holy Spirit. There can be lots of helpful "support specialists" along the way, like mentors, grandparents, books, and videos, but all you really need is Him. He loves your child even more than you do; after all, He does have a vested interest! Once you have the proper perspective on being a parent, you should naturally desire to do the best job possible. It's like a gift back to God. And He wants you to succeed! Parenting can be fun and rewarding, which I happen to believe is the way God intended for it to be. That is exactly why He gave you tools to assist you.

Over the years I have learned (often the hard way) that my personal walk with the Lord directly affected my parenting. When I was where I should be with the Lord, I had much more understanding about what I was supposed to do. When I was drifting, careless, or just going through the motions, I would make often make decisions that weren't the best. Notice I didn't say that the walk with the Lord made parenting easy. Parenting isn't always easy. Some decisions are tough to make.

Following through on consequences for misbehavior probably can't be classified as fun or easy. I am not equating my relationship with Christ to a genie in a bottle for parenting. I am merely saying that the wisdom, perseverance, and desire for parenting are directly correlated with my time alone with Him and how well I listened to His voice. How can I desire to get to the heart of my child when my own heart isn't yielded to the Savior? What makes me think I will make the right decision if I failed to ask him to guide me that morning? How will I have patience to discipline correctly when I haven't sought forgiveness for my own sin before Him?

I am fairly confident that each generation has viewed the next one as more wicked and perverse than their current generation. The New Testament describes the cycle of the reprobate mind and how sin builds and builds until it escalates out of control. I have watched over the years as my own daughters struggled with the same issues in middle school that I dealt with in high school. Words and suggestive language, which never would have been uttered in an average home, are now commonplace on television and in the movies, so much so that we do not even give them a second thought. The demoralization of our culture has had a profound effect upon our children, and unfortunately, upon their hearts. Parenting is tough, but what better place to gain strength and get our marching orders than from sitting at His feet and immersing ourselves in His Word? Remember, He gave you your children as a gift, and He has a vested interest in your success, so He gave you the tools. Walk with Him and let Him guide you. As I look back over my journey as a mom, I can guarantee that I made mistakes when my heart was not where it should have been.

While the title of Mom came easy (well, maybe your labor and delivery was far from easy), one day you were just given the title. Your gift from God might have been a complete surprise, or you might have been like Hannah, Rachel, or Sarah who waited years for a child. For most moms, however, being a mom just happened, you didn't have to do a whole lot to get there. (Trust me, I'm not discounting the stretch marks that remained even though you went through three jars of cocoa butter, or your hours of labor while your husband watched television.) For many, all of the sudden you were a mom. Parenting, on the other hand, doesn't just happen. In order to reach your child's heart, you must be very intentional. I am not referring to the color you selected for the nursery, or the name you carefully chose for your baby. I am talking about daily, deliberate, and conscious decisions as a mom to reach your child's heart for as long as they have breath.

This means being aware of what is going on in life's daily circumstances, so that you can seize teachable moments. This requires time—time spent doing what your children are doing and listening to what they are saying. Understand what and how they are processing. Since you are already prayed up before the Lord, when the moments arise (I promise you they will), you will be ready to make optimum value out of a situation. One of our favorite movies when the girls were younger was *Pollyanna*. In the story, a darling young orphan steals the heart of everyone in the town with her eternal optimism and encouraging ways. When our girls were little, we would play the "glad game" which Pollyanna teaches in the movie. If something happened that was not to their liking (it could be little or big), they would have to list the things about it that made them glad. I have to chuckle, because as they grew older, one sibling would begin to encourage another, and she would respond, "That's enough, Pollyanna!" I can laugh because they understood the concept. No normal eight-year-old is going to come home from gym class and play the glad game because they were chosen last for kick ball. They just don't do that on their own. When the first young male breaks a promise he made to your 16-year-old daughter, she is not naturally going to list all the good things about that broken promise. After five boxes of tissues and hours of listening to her cry, then it might begin to be time for you to intentionally try to reach her heart.

Reaching their hearts isn't a once-and-done concept either. Have you ever committed the same sin more than one time? As adults, we don't always get it the first time around. Neither do our children. Reaching their hearts, even on one particular issue, often involves more than one round. Patience is required, and we must continue to be intentional. One of our daughters was injured in a game her senior year in high school. She played all three seasons for her school but the injury was so extensive and required surgery, which meant she missed two seasons her senior year. As captain, she had to sit on the bench after she was mobile enough to even get to the games. We had choices to make. Either she wallowed in her self-pity and nursed bitterness, or she accepted the injury that God allowed to happen and made the best of it.

Now let me rewind the clock for the purpose of illustration. Six years prior, in middle school (same sport, by the way), she suffered a less complicated, but similar injury. Rehab, crutches, surgery, wheelchair… we had it all for about six months. This is my social child, who had to sit on the porch and watch her friends play volleyball in the backyard. She had to sit on the sidelines for youth group, school activities, and everything else. My happy, outgoing, and lively daughter became nasty and bitter. The mom in me thought I had done everything I could to help her through this trial. I had purchased her a pretty journal, and we started to make a journal entry each day on where we saw God working. I was attempting to redirect her heart on a daily basis. Many a night we wept for her and lifted her heart up to the Lord. We didn't appear to reach her that time. It broke my heart.

Six years later, she found herself at the same crossroads. This time, the situation was more intense. Missing out on her senior year? Losing activities that she loved and potentially even her senior trip? This occurred at the same time she was applying for colleges. One day I was cleaning up the piles of papers on the dining room table when I ran across her application essay. She talked about her injury and the "loss" of her senior year. She went on to describe how she was determined to handle it correctly this time, because she blew it last time. Yes, she was going to miss out on tons of "fun," but in light of reality, what she was missing was not what mattered; how she handled it was what mattered. Tears of joy poured down my cheeks as I read what she had written. We had reached her heart; it just took years to show. That writing was in the early stages of her injury; this was a nine-month recovery. Did she stay home and wallow in self-pity? Not this time. She went out as soon as I would let her, desiring to make the most of it. This time around, when folks came to cheer her up or take her out to lunch during a long week, they would tell me, "I came to encourage her, and I was the one who was encouraged!" Praise be to God! Reaching your child's heart takes time, and it has to be intentional. Do not grow wearing in well doing, dear Mom. Press on and be intentional. It is worth the persistence and tears on your part.

What motivates your children? What drives them? They learn that lovely word "mine" at such a young age; do you think they will just grow out of using that word? Do you think they will naturally learn to think of others more important than themselves? Obviously that doesn't happen; Scripture has to command us to put others first. If it has to be commanded, then I hardly think it is something that we do naturally on our own. Our children were born thinking only of themselves, and if we don't direct their heart, they will continue to do so. It's really quite simple. Either intervene and redirect, or raise a self-focused, self-absorbed young adult. The choice is yours!

This is for exciting and rewarding situations, too, not just the difficult ones. What about dating? How do you handle your teenagers' relationships with the opposite sex? If we were all polled, we would probably come up with a variety of answers from one end of the spectrum to the other. Some parents choose to let their teenagers go out on a date – alone with their date – unmonitored, as young as middle school. Others choose not to allow their teen to be alone with a member of the opposite sex until after the age of 18. Whatever the policy is in your house, my encouragement would be to mentor their heart in the process. I wanted my daughters to have the opportunity to be out on a date (alone) with a young man before they went away to college because I wanted to deal with their heart through the process. As a family, we had dating standards and guidelines that must be followed. It wasn't *cart blanche* go out with whomever, whenever, wherever. But, throughout the process we made sure to deal with their hearts. Intentional parenting involves so many aspects of your child's life.

One of our daughters is very much into basketball. I tell people she was born dribbling a basketball. There came a point in her high school career where she had to decide who she was playing for. Was she playing for herself? Her dad? Her coach? College coaches? Where was her heart—because ultimately the answer to that question would direct the outcome. She decided she was playing for an audience of One. That was her slogan, and it went on her wrist at every game. She had to consciously remind herself of that before every game; she became intentional with that. It didn't just happen. She had to get her own heart to the right place. It's the same with parenting. As a mom, if you do not consciously seek to reach your child's heart, I promise you the enemy will. Do not make the mistake of thinking that because you are a believer, or because you attend church or Bible study, or because your child goes to youth group or even a Christian school, that their heart will be fine. I'm trying to scream—I know that's not very nice, but please—it's your job, and if you don't do it, someone else will. If you get nothing out else of my chapter, please retain this. If you are not intentional about getting your child's heart, it won't happen. The enemy will win.

That leads me right into my next encouragement. Moms, do not worry about what you are missing while you are busy trying to reach your child's heart. Parenting is far more important than a book club, girls' night out, or a weekend away. Those things are not bad; I'm not implying that. But even good choices and good activities are not the best choice if they take up our time so that we cannot be with our children. I firmly believe in dating your husband, and when your house is full of toddlers and young children, you need to get out for some adult time. I also believe parenting is a joint venture; please spend time alone with your spouse discussing your parenting decisions. We lead busy lives and if we are not careful, we can be involved in so many good things that the best things never come to fruition. Don't worry about what may be out there that you aren't seeing. But be sure your priorities are straight.

No one understands the balancing act more than I. We chose for me to work outside of the home full time for many years while our daughters were growing up. I worked so that they could have the benefits of attending a Christian school. (I'm not elevating any particular choice above another—this is for the purposes of illustration.) Because we made this choice, I was not with the children 24/7. For us, that meant that I did not choose to do all the other things that often women do. For example, my husband teaches every Monday night. I have been home with our kids every Monday night since they were small. I wanted to seize moments and intentionally planned to do so. If we need to plan a date night, we look at the calendar and pick a night when the kids have a commitment when possible. Don't throw the baby out with the bathwater; I'm not saying I am with my girls every moment. I am saying I was home with them a lot more than most because we chose to invest our time that way. My empty nest is right around the corner, and then I will have the time to enjoy lots of "good" things. As a mom, be cautious of loading up with too many good things that you don't have time for the best things. They will be gone sooner than you can ever imagine; invest while they are under your roof.

This would be the time where, if I was actually sharing this lesson in a teaching setting, I would wave a red flag. In fact, I might even be tempted to move throughout the room, waving it furiously so that everyone knew I was sharing a warning. The red flag has one word written on it: "Hypocrisy." Sadly, through lessons learned by my own mistakes and by watching others, I firmly believe the number one thing that attacks what we are trying to do as a parent, and often negates what we might have accomplished, is our hypocrisy as moms. I can share my heart, invest in theirs, and make strides. But when my kids see hypocrisy in my life, I have just undone what I have tried to do. I have seen this time and time again. Sadly, many moms fail to consider this important aspect in parenting. Of course, we know what Scripture says about hypocrites, and we strive not to be one. But have we really examined ourselves and our own hearts for hypocrisy? I found it had to be an intentional (I think that's a buzz word for this book) and daily part of my life. I had to fall on my face before a Holy God and ask Him to expose hypocrisy in my life to me. And I have to deal with it then and there. What good does it do to nurture my daughter's heart in peer relationships during those difficult middle school adolescent years, and then sit and have a cup of coffee with a girlfriend and "discuss" other women? Everyone knows the saying "more is caught than taught," which is very true. But we need to expand that thought a little bit more. If I am seeking to nurture and guide their hearts in the ways of the Lord, what am I doing about my own heart?

Yes, I've gone full circle with my thoughts. It begins and ends for me with my own heart. I believe that the number one area we women tend to overlook is our own hearts, specifically in the area of hypocrisy. For example, when our kids come home from school with a bad grade or a discipline notice, if we fly off the handle and blast the teacher, or even if we quietly disagree and tell our child "we'll take care of that," we have just limited the impact this teacher can have on our child. We have subconsciously told our child, "Don't obey the teacher; he doesn't know what he is doing." Did you really mean to say that? Probably not. I cannot imagine wanting to be a hypocrite to my children. But if I am not alert and watching for danger, then I can easily find myself in that camp.

I love parenting so much that if I could, I would turn the clock back and do it all over again. Are there things I would do differently? Sure. But that is not the main reason I want to go back. I loved it all; I will forever be grateful to the Lord for the privilege of being a mom. I am honored and humbled that He chose me for such a task. If you are reading this book, perhaps the entire task is ahead of you. Perhaps you are almost finished, or maybe you are struggling. Whatever your situation, I pray you will see your task as a God-given blessing, realize that He gave you what you need to complete the task, and that you commit to be one intentional mom.

When Parents Go After the Heart

Intentionally going after the hearts of your children can seem like a fruitless task sometimes, but you never know how much impact even the small things have. Perhaps it would be helpful to hear that from the children themselves.

From Jessica

Growing up in a home where my parents went after my heart for God was stretching and tough at times, but it was worth it. There were moments in my childhood when I wished I could change their desire for me to love the Lord and to strive to be a godly young lady. But they never gave up, and I want to share some of the ways they reached me.

The first would have been how a discipline issue was handled. We would sit down and talk about it, and Dad would always come down to what was in my heart. I even remember times when I did something wrong and would need a spanking; he would talk with me about why I was being spanked, pray with me, spank me, and then hold me while I cried. (Sometimes, the tears were coming down his face as well.) At the end of the issue, it would boil down to what is in my heart.

Secondly, Dad never missed an opportunity to ask what I was doing in my devotions or what I was learning from my devotions. Dad always challenged me to continue growing and striving to know God more. At dinner we would have devotions followed by dad asking us what we were doing in out quiet time with God. He would say "How is your quiet time going?" I will admit that many times I was embarrassed to tell him I hadn't been doing well that week, but it would just make me work harder the next week. Even though at times it frustrated me and I felt as if they were being controlling, it only helped deepen my desire for the Lord.

Thirdly, Mom and Dad modeled service for me. There were times I missed a birthday party, athletic event, or gathering due to church or a service activity. Even though there were times I wasn't happy with their choice, I learned through it that serving Christ needed to be a priority in my life.

As I reflect on my parents and how they chose to go after my heart for God, I realize what an opportunity and blessing I had to grow up in that environment. I wouldn't change any of it. I am not sure words can express how thankful I am that they never gave up. I believe with everything I have that I would not be here today if my mother and father had not gone after my heart. Many of the friends whom I grew up with are away from the Lord and not living their lives for Him. Many of them didn't have parents who went after their hearts for God. But mine did, and for that reason I am very thankful.

From Jennifer

For years I saved a special voicemail that said, "Happy Valentine's Day! I just wanted to remind you that if nobody tells you today that they love you, it doesn't matter because I love you and that's all that matters." That message was from my daddy, and it was so meaningful, mostly because I knew it was true. If there is one thing that I can say was one of the most important things about growing up in a Christian home, it was love. This is not to say that only Christian homes have love, but I do believe that Christian homes can reflect true love—God's love. My parents showed love, each in their own way, to their daughters and to each other. There was never a doubt in my mind that my parents loved me or my sisters. Their love had many different forms, but it was constant. Love was spoken through words of praise and encouragement, and also through wisdom and counsel. Love was demonstrated through sacrifices and discipline.

One of the most wonderful illustrations in Scripture is God as our Heavenly Father and the love He has for His children. I was able to grasp that concept because I understood the love that I experienced from my Christian parents. Because my parents loved me, I learned to trust and respect them. I have an understanding of love because I have experienced love and I know that God's love is even deeper. I am blessed to have both parents who love the Lord and lead by wonderful example. They told me they loved me, and they showed it. They told me God loved me and I learned to see, trust, and believe in that love. I am not a parent, but I am the product of a loving home, and I would encourage parents to never underestimate the power of loving your child, and showing them that love.

From Kirsten

Looking back on my youth, I see how my parents truly went after my heart. Whenever I did wrong, they used it as a teaching moment rather than a time to just yell and punish. I remember one instant when I was in trouble, and my parents and I were sitting on the stairs. I was very upset at myself for doing the wrong thing, and they talked to me about the choice I had made. They showed me a choice that was a better option, which had never occurred to me. So although I did wrong and got punished, they showed me what to do the next time the conflict arose.

Each time I did something wrong, I was always told the right choice to make next time; thus providing me with the skill to better determine the correct choice when different challenges confronted me. I'm so thankful that my parents went after my heart and showed me my mistakes rather than just punishing me and not explaining the different choices I had.

From Katelyn

What with being the youngest child, and a twin, I found myself getting into trouble often. You know the song "Bad to the Bone?" Yeah, that was my theme song. I really cannot count all the times I got in trouble or even tell you what I did, but I can tell you what my parents did every time. Sometimes it was a spoon, sometimes it was a ruler, or something like that. But every time I was punished, I can remember my mom or dad sitting with me and talking with me about what I did. They wanted to know why I did it, and what I could have done instead. Then they would explain to me why it was wrong and what they expected me to do next time. I feel like that is just one of the ways they were going after my heart. You see they are not the parents that just send you to the corner for five minutes and when it is up they act like nothing has happened;

they want to know your intentions and your thoughts. They cared more about why I did something than what I did. Of course, as a child I did not understand why they would do it, but looking back now I am so thankful that they took the time to go after my heart.

One of the best things my mother did for me was to call me out when I had a horrible attitude. When I was in sixth grade, I was injured during a basketball game. I tore my meniscus and had to go to therapy for months before and after my surgery. I was in a wheelchair and on crutches for a very long time. Of course, in the beginning I loved all the attention and gifts. But after the second week I was tired of it all. My attitude switched to that of a grumpy, snotty little girl. I remember my mother sitting down at the table with me and saying, "Kate, you have a horrible attitude about this situation. One day you will heal and walk normally again, but there are many others out there who won't." You know, attitude reflects the heart, and my mother was making sure my heart was better than my attitude showed. After our talk, I went upstairs and rededicated my life to Christ. I am so thankful my mother was looking at my heart; she did not just baby me and try to make me feel better. She called me out and helped me get back on track.

16

Help for the Hurting Parent

IT IS EASY AFTER reading a book like this to become discouraged. That was certainly not my intention, but for some it may be the outcome. Please forgive because I only want to help parents be the best that they can be. After observing and experiencing parenting over the last 25 years, I have become burdened over the needs of the family. We are losing far too many of our children, and I want to help in some way to restore the order to the home. Please accept these feeble attempts at trying to assist, not discourage. My prayer is that this chapter will refresh you and renew your hope.

Principles to Help Your Parenting

There are many principles that help give us an eternal perspective on our parenting mission. They all involve God's view of our task. I hope you take some encouragement from them!

Principle #1: *God loves these children more than we do*. Sometimes as parents we think that no one loves our children like we do. We are mistaken. God so loved them that He gave His Son to die for them. We need to remember that He desires the best for our children, far beyond what we could even imagine or think. And that leads me to the next principle.

Principle #2: *God gave them the best home for them*. Now I am sure that someone is going to take issue with this, but you have to keep in mind the sovereignty of God. Does God do anything that is not good? Thinking that God isn't fair or right means you don't believe He is sovereign or that he loves you. Children are a gift from God, and would He place children in your home without a reason and purpose? Now, there are difficult things in life and things that are hard for us to understand.

But God's ways are above our ways, and His thoughts are above our thoughts (Is 55:9). To assume we know best is to do a disservice to God and His sovereign control over all.

Principle #3: *We live in a fallen and sinful world, and sometimes things happen that are as a result of evil.* Because of this evil, children are born in situations and circumstances that were never intended to be. Some might say, "Why doesn't God stop the suffering of children? Why does God allow such things? What kind of God would allow such to happen?" God does not cause these things, and He only "permits" them because humanity has brought these things upon itself. And when we bring these things upon ourselves, God permits them to happen. When adults do sinful things and God deals with them, sometimes the innocent suffer. When a nation's leadership brings war to their soil, innocent people will suffer. When a drunken father drives home at night, sometimes innocent children in his car suffer and sometimes even those in other cars. When a mom smokes during pregnancy, the innocent baby in the womb suffers. We may feel that only those who do the sin ought to suffer for the sin, but God set this discipline in motion long before us. Adam sinned, and therefore every person who is born after Adam has to die. You may not like God's rules, but God's rules are always right and glorifying to Him, whether we agree or not. Can I make sense out of the fact that babies suffer by being brought into homes that abuse them? Can I make sense out of the thousands of abortions where babies were torn apart and suffered in the mother's womb? Can I make sense out of the orphans, homeless, sex-traded, and other horrific scenarios for children? No, I cannot. But there are things about God that are not easily understood and things about life that often perplex us (Deut. 29:29). Circumstances and situations do not change what is theologically accurate in God's Word. Trusting God is all about believing that He knows best and is sovereign over all. I believe that in the end we all will see that our God is just who He says He is, and we can trust Him.

Principle #4: *There is no such thing as a parent who cannot be a good parent.* Just as I don't believe that there are children who cannot be good, I also do not accept that there are parents who cannot be good. Now some children behave badly, and so do some parents. But God is able to make any parent into a good parent and any child into a good child. The problem is the rebellious heart. We have the potential to be excellent parents if we place our faith and trust in Christ and walk according to the Scriptures. The choice is ours. And the reason we don't behave as good parents comes down to our choices. As long as God is left out of our lives we are going to struggle to be a good parent. Even if you have failed for years, God is still able to take those years and repair them. One of the coolest parts of the future of the earth is that our Lord is going to rule on this earth for 1,000 years during the Millennial Kingdom. During this time He is going to restore the earth to its original form, the Garden of Eden. He will take all the smog, the pollution, all the erosion, all the garbage, and make it into the perfect world that He first gave to man. If God can do that for this fallen earth, surely He can do so for fallen man who He loves dearly. And certainly He can help restore the years where our parenting was lacking. How big is your God?

Now I am sure there is some parent out there who feels like such a failure that they have already determined that they are such a bad parent that there is no use in trying. They blame all their children's bad behavior on themselves or their mate, and they see no reason to even try any more. I can certainly understand the despair. I have seen it enough in many other parents and the pain is so great that it seems better to just quit than to keep trying and fail. Most parents fight that temptation at one time or another. But just as God can take a sinner and make him into a saint, He can take struggling parents and make them into parents that are models for others to learn from. Yes, you can be that parent. Don't lose hope. And always remember that God judges parents on a whole different scale than the world does. Our goal is to hear "well done" from Him and not from the world.

Principle #5: *There is no such thing as a hopeless case.* Far too often we throw up our hands and give up on our parenting, our marriage, our family, or our children. But for every one who gives up, there is a story of hope: people saw God take that which appeared hopeless, and turn it into that which is amazing. But is that not what God is all about—taking that which seems impossible and making something amazing out of it? We need to learn to forget the past and learn from its lessons, rather than allow the past to control our view of the future. Your situation cannot be helpless and hopeless when the Lord is on your side! See the next section for a little more help in this area.

Principle #6: *Stop trying to do it your way and put your full faith in God.* When you do it all your own way, you will soon find out that it doesn't exactly produce good results. When are you going to stop trying to do it in your own strength and turn it all over to the Lord? Applying Biblical principles has incredible results, and I would doubt at this point in your agony that you have much to lose. The worst that could happen by parenting God's way is that you would know you are pleasing Him. Doing things God's way does not mean you are going to turn everything around overnight. Just as the rebellion did not occur over night, neither will the recovery. It took time for rebellion to creep in, and it will take time for rebellion to leave. Going after the heart will take much time and prayer, but God is able to do amazing things with even a McDonald's Happy Meal.

But Wait . . . What if I Have Already Failed?

As I noted above, the answer is God. If there were no God, you would only have luck to rely on. I don't believe in luck, but I do believe in a God who can do "exceedingly abundantly above all we can ask or think" (Eph. 3:20–21). That is not luck; that is faith.

I'm sure you have figured out the pattern by now. A vital situation requires vital and immediate prayer. You may have a situation that seems hopeless, but we have a God who is the God of the hopeless. Prayer does work and God mends many broken lives. Just today, when returning from a hospital visit, I stopped on the interstate prior to my exit and picked up a man who was walking with a gas can. I had just passed his truck and could see he was in need of some help. I don't recommend this for everyone, but the Lord just pulled me to the side of the road and I believed it was of His leading to do so. The man had a several-mile walk both ways and surely could use some assistance. Little did I realize that his greatest need would be spiritual. As we headed down the road, I told him that I believed that God had led me to pick him up and maybe God was reaching out to him. He agreed and said that he had gone through a divorce and he had drifted away from God. He used to be in church and even had kids in a Christian school. The divorce sent him spiraling down and he needed to get back on track. Here was a man who had "failed" the last several years of his life and the children were the ones who were suffering the most. I explained that he needed to go back and first get right with God and then see what God is about to do in His life. My point is that God is the great Healer. He may just want to do a mighty miracle through you for His glory.

Remember that you cannot dwell in the past. Paul talked about forgetting those things which are behind and pressing on to the things ahead (Phil 3:13). So you have failed in the past. If there is need of reconciliation or recompense, then do it. You may have to ask forgiveness from a child, a mate, or someone else involved. If those things cannot be fixed, don't dwell there. There may be cause to sit down with your pastor or some other trusted counselor who can guide you through the dark waters of the past and give you guidance about the future. God puts our sins in the sea of forgetfulness and as far as the East is from the West (Ps 103:12). He has no desire to drag up our past and cripple our future. If the past is being brought regularly to your attention, it is not the Lord that is doing it.

Regardless of the feelings or hurts from the past, begin to Biblically love your children. Maybe you have never expressed this love very well before. Maybe you have been anything but a loving parent. Maybe your children want to have nothing to do with you. Don't leave it there. I would suggest attempting to meet with them and confess your failures, ask for forgiveness, and try to start fresh. It will take some time, so start slowly, but hopefully your humility will open some doors. Don't say "if I have hurt you…" when you know you have wronged them. Just be straight with them. If they won't meet with you, write them a letter. Have a trusted friend read it first, but send a letter doing the same as you would do face to face. Genuine repentance is right regardless of the results, and God resists the proud but gives grace to the humble.

As you stay in prayer, know that God will guide you every step of the way. The steps of a good man are ordered by the Lord (Ps 37:23), so let Him lead and guide. Remember that He is a great Healer; just ask those in the Gospels who had been ill for years when God made them completely whole. Those who had never walked could now run and jump with no therapy. That God of the New Testament is the same yesterday, today, and forever. He did it for the lame and blind, and He could do it for you.

It is time to exercise faith, because without faith it is impossible to please Him. As you put your faith in action, watch the God of action go to work. When something is left in His hands, then He has full access to it. Put yourself, your parenting, and your children in His hands by faith and let Him do the impossible. Don't stop believing in a miracle-working God. The Bible is full of amazing miracles and over 40 years of walking with the Savior, I have seen far too many to mention. Whatever happens, don't lose faith.

As a follower of Jesus Christ, I have to often admit that I don't measure up. When Jesus Christ is our Example, it is easy to fall short. He is a tough standard for comparison! And when it comes to parenting, we have our Heavenly Father to measure up to as well. Ouch! Is there any wonder we often want to castigate ourselves for behavior that is just not what a God-fearing man or woman ought to do?

But I am not interested in the bad side of our walk. Our Lord knows we are not going to measure up to the standards He set for us and He readily applies and supplies grace in the time of need. If parenting was about perfection, then we should all sit around the campfire and sing our final song. Parenting is just as much about learning from our mistakes as it is about avoiding mistakes.

Parents take heart: God did not give those children to you because He knew you were going to be perfect. He gave them to you as an act of His mercy and grace. Enjoy the best of it and learn to grow through the pains. You will come forth as gold when the refining is over. In that pure picture of gold, our Savior can be best seen. Shine, dear saint of God, and be all you can be for His glory. Remember: His love is not conditional.

17

A Word to the Children

Parents, my goal is for your children to read these pages. I am concerned for our children today, especially those in Christian families. You could have them read the entire book if you wish, but particularly I would hope that many children would read this chapter as a message from my heart to them. (Read the chapter first yourself. This is directed primarily at the youth.) These are the kinds of things that I wished someone would have told me when I was young so that I could have avoided some of the stupid things I did as a youth.

Parents Are for Your Protection

PARENTS HAVE BEEN GIVEN to you by God for your protection. When a parent makes a decision their child cannot understand, and it works out for good, it often surprises the child! You see, God is the One who takes the authority and uses it for His glory and the protection of those under that authority.

I am sure that there are times when your parents have messed up, but there are also numerous stories where parents said no to something that the child wanted to do, and the child was spared something horrific. It only takes one such time to help a child realize that parents are here for their protection. Sometimes, parents just have this sense about something or someone, even if they cannot explain it. And they should not have to explain it. There are probably times that an explanation would be helpful, but you can't justify rebellion just because you don't understand something.

A Word to the Children

Of course, as I look back over my childhood years, there were times my parents said no to something that just did not set well with me at that time. I am sure I was not pleasant about my frustration, but I believe that my parents spared me from much heartache over the years. I also believe that I would not be a pastor today had they not been firm with me when they sensed a concern. If your parents have backbone enough to say no to something that they think will harm you, that's terrific! I guarantee you will appreciate it in the future!

Parents Are Not as Dumb as You Think!

When you are born and throughout your young years, your parents are wise, kind, and caring. Often, however, when you become a teenager, suddenly your parents become complete idiots! I have seen this over and over again. I have seen this in the way some teens talk to their parents. It is sad and painful to observe. It is almost as if a clock goes off and teens become smart and parents lose their wisdom. But parents haven't lost their brains; the only things that have changed are your perceptions.

I just want to encourage you teens especially to avoid such an erroneous way of thinking. It certainly does not help that many of your friends are doing these kinds of things and that most of the television shows also reveal the same ideas: parents are not very smart. Even the music of the day will take every opportunity to slam the parents. If you follow the same line of thinking, you will hinder a major source of wisdom and knowledge that you have daily at your fingertips.

Now that does not mean that parents are always right. But I can imagine the look of shock that might be in the average teen's mind when they hear that there was actually a show years ago called *Father Knows Best*. Parents are not perfect, and they will make mistakes. Some parents don't even attempt to be good parents. But with all that being said, remember that parents are the best source of earthly wisdom that you will find. Make every effort to listen to your parents and learn from their knowledge. By doing so, you will save yourself much heartache!

We Live in Rebellious Days

Rebellion is a big concern in the home. God has no tolerance for rebellion! In the Old Testament, rebellious adults were punished severely, even to the point of death. And—this may surprise you—rebellious children were also to be taken to the elders and put to death (Deut 28:18–21). God has very little patience with rebellion. His Word says that rebellion is just as bad as the sin of witchcraft. He takes it seriously.

Defying Mom and Dad is a very serious act that you may want to reconsider. By the way; have you ever thought about just how much rebellion (not doing what you are told to do or doing what you were told not to do) makes you a rebellious child? Does one act of rebellion make you rebellious? Does two acts? Does it matter as to what the situation is? Who gets to decide when you are actually rebellious? Is that your call, your parents' call, or God's call?

We are living in rebellious times, and many young people believe it is certainly permissible, if not the rite of passage, to stretch their wings and be rebellious to some level. We even have a name for it: teenage rebellion. That has become such a common phrase that it is often expected. No, you don't have to sow your wild oats, and you can have an excellent relationship with your parents as a teen! Why suffer through all the anger and heartache your friends are going through?

Every rebellious act (not doing what you are told to do or doing what you were told not to do) is an affront to a Holy God and will not go unnoticed. Adolescent rebellion even sets the foundation for future rebellion that could become part of the lifestyle of you as an adult. Taking rebellion lightly is similar to trying to raise a pet rattlesnake. It may go on tame for a while, but eventually it will bite and spread its venom. That is what rebellion is—venom. It poisons relationships and destroys peace.

Too many children and parents do not see just how damaging rebellion is to the cause of Christ and the family. Just take the time to do a study of rebellion in the Old Testament. Watch how nation after nation was destroyed, how Satan fell, and how God's own people were severely disciplined because of their rebellious hearts. We live in a very rebellious age, and you must be careful that you are not being conformed to this world. Romans 12:1–2 reminds us that the world wants to squeeze us into its mold. Be warned that Satan is a rebellious being and desires a rebellious following. When you rebel, you are acting out in Satanic fashion. Is this what you want? Here is a thought: live for your God and parents as you want your kids to live for you when you are a parent.

Don't Compare Your Parents with Someone Else's Parents

I remember comparing parents often when I was a child; I would wish I had someone else's parents. And it was always about the fact that they allowed their child to do something I was not allowed to do. My parents were very strict. I didn't really appreciate that while I was a child, but I can only shout the praises of God about it today. My parents realized how children can rebel and they were determined that I was not going to be another statistic. Praise God they were faithful.

I grew up in a very small community where everyone knows everybody and everybody's business. I was fortunate to have many classmates who lived just a short distance from my house. On any given day, I had at least 10 possible friends who were just minutes away. All of these were friends who could be reached via the old way of travel called walking. It was not uncommon to have that many in our yard playing all kinds of sports. Our yard was the community play yard with basketball and other sports based on the season. But not all of my friends grew up in Christian homes, and therefore the standards for each family were somewhat different, even among the believers. As I grew older, it was more difficult to hear how my friends went to that party, or went to that gathering, or hung out at someone's house, all of which I was forbidden to go to or do. I remember that even when I was allowed to date, many times the girl could stay out later than I could! Of course, I would never let anyone know that; it was embarrassing. Oh, to have different parents who weren't so strict! Yet I look today at many of my friends in that inner circle and I see that few of them follow Jesus. Some have broken homes and messed up lives, and some are even wasting their last years.

Looking back, I would not trade all that "embarrassment" for where I am today. And I suspect that many of my friends, upon looking back, would like to have had parents like mine. I just didn't see it then, and doubt many of you will see it today. You may just have to trust me on this one.

The funny thing is, children on both sides of the parenting pendulum often wish they had parents on the other side! Some wish their parents were more strict, because it would show that they care, and some wish their parents were more lenient. You come to the conclusion that very few children are satisfied with their parental standards. One day you will be a parent and you may be surprised to find out just how many of your parents' "stupid" and "unfair" rules you will apply!

The Sovereign God has given to you by His divine selection and choice and for your good the exact parents on earth that you need. If you believe differently, you are greatly mistaken. God gives children to parents and He loves you more than you will ever know on this side. If you were God, wouldn't you give each child the best parent for their personality? Then why doubt His methods or ways? You have been given the best parents possible to make you the best children possible and to grow up to be the best adults possible. Sin greatly interferes with the process, but that does not negate the actions of the sovereign God that we have.

Be an Example, Even if Your Parents Are Not

Far too often children have used their parents as an excuse for their own behavior. Dad does not go to church, so why should I? Mom smokes cigarettes and does not want us to smoke, but why can't I? Dad does not obey the traffic laws, so what difference does it make if I cheat at school? Dad and Mom talk about the pastor behind his back, so what difference does it make if I do the same? Dad never reads his Bible, so why should I? Mom is a hypocrite, so what difference does it make? And of course the list goes on and on.

Using your parents as an excuse for your own unspiritual behavior will not be acceptable when you stand before the Lord. Parents often need to do a better job of living out their faith in front of their children. Hypocrisy and ungodliness is just not appropriate, but unfortunately, it happens. There are parents who are poor role models for their own children. But this isn't a good reason to be an ungodly person yourself.

You see, each individual will give an account of his/her life. On that fateful day, none of us will be able to excuse our behavior because of another person. It is unfortunate that many young people today have poor examples lived before them. Sometimes the poor examples extend beyond the immediate family to grandparents, aunts/uncles, cousins, and many more. They also may have poor examples by youth pastors,

Sunday School teachers, and others who have some form of leadership over them. Yet the ungodliness of these examples should not cause you to drift into their lifestyle and behavior. They will have to give account before God, the same as you. They have chosen to live as a hypocrite, but you don't have to choose the same. If you have bad examples in front of you, find good ones! There are good examples out there, and you may just have to search a little harder. Find someone in spiritual leadership who is a good role model and begin to see how they walk and live. And never forget that man is going to fail you, but Jesus never fails. He is our ultimate example and we should never allow others cloud out His example to us.

Another area where parents are often bad examples is the area of favoritism. Far too many parents favor one child over another. You will need to just accept that this problem does exist, do all you can to correct it humbly, and do not let it destroy your path of growth. Favoritism exists also in the world outside the family and God may be getting you ready for things that at this early age you cannot see. God does not waste any circumstance or situations. Believe that God is preparing you for something far bigger than this! The journey you are going through now, though it may be painful, will be worth it in the end!

Keep Yourself Pure from the World

Just as we also live in a very rebellious age, we also live in a very immoral time. I wonder if these just don't go together because most rebellious children also become promiscuous. You have to determine, as Joseph and Daniel in the Bible, to not defile yourselves with the temptations of this world.

There is no question that you are going to be bombarded with much in the area of immorality. Just about every secular television show, movie, or music video will have some kind of deviant behavior or lewd scene. I have been amazed over the last few years how Hollywood has continued to push the gay agenda, by quietly showcasing a gay person, making him out to be one of the coolest people in the show. Everyone loves this person and he often displays a love for all and is a great person and citizen. When the last time a Christian was given that kind of cool presentation? I would never have dreamed that in my lifetime I would have seen this kind of a turnaround in the area of values.

I Heart Parenting

Portraying anyone with a sinful lifestyle was strictly inappropriate just a few years ago. Now it is flaunted in front of us on a regular basis and we are expected to receive and approve of this lifestyle. Never do they show the effects of any sinful behaviors: the liver disease that comes from alcohol, the cancer that comes from smoking, the broken homes that come from affairs, the diseases that come from heterosexual and homosexual lifestyles, the pain of a girl who faces post-abortion syndrome. They show the pleasure in sin for a season, but never the pain that follows such sinful behavior.

You need to determine now that you are going to keep yourself unspotted by the world. It won't be cool, and you may be talked about and laughed at. But as you walk down the aisle as a pure virgin, you can wear the white dress with the full confidence of an obedient child of God. And young man, as you wait for her to walk the aisle, you can hold her hand with dignity knowing that you will be with your love for the first time that night and the first girl ever. Pre-marital and extra-marital sex is extremely harmful. The statistics are very high of those who get involved sexually before marriage end up in divorce. Keep yourself pure.

And much care ought to be given to what is acceptable in a physical relationship before marriage. How far is appropriate for a couple before they are married? Because of the nature of such a book, I cannot address this in its entirety, but let me give you a few suggestions. First, at no time should your hand be placed on a portion of the body that remains covered in public. Second, at no time should you allow someone to see any part of your body that is considered the private areas. Third, at no time should you be lying down beside one another before you are married. Fourth, at no time should you be alone and involved in prolonged kissing or caressing. Continued behavior like this has only one final destination. There is no reason to stay out late and no reason to be alone in one another's homes without parental supervision. Finally, when in public, if you are expressing physical affection, there is a strong chance you are going further in private. What message are you sending?

I would also suggest you put together dating standards and hand them into your parents. Let your dating friend also see them. These are standards that you have made before God and need to keep with all diligence. Have your parents look over them and discuss them with you. Make these standards a serious part of your life. Don't put yourself in compromising situations. One mistake made in this area could affect

A Word to the Children

seriously the rest of your life. And I am not just talking about a pregnancy. There are other areas such as disease that need to be considered. Plus, I can affirm to you that if you go too far with someone physically, it will be told to a friend of theirs. If you break up with this person, others will certainly hear of it. You will become a person sought out for the wrong reasons. Once you give in physically to a certain level, more levels will be explored in subsequent dates. The physical drive will not stay content with just small adventures. The ultimate prize will drive the individual more than you understand, and if you believe you are in love, it will be hard to resist. By the way girls, if you have not heard this saying before, let it sink in: boys don't mind being in the antiquing business, but when it comes to buying (marriage), they don't like used furniture.

Another concern about keeping yourself pure involves the areas of pornography. This sinful material is so available to people today that it is alarming. Children of young ages are being exposed to pictures and actions that should never leave the private bedroom. Once you begin to taste of this world, it will be hard to go back to pure thinking. Make sure you have proper safeguards in place. Never access a computer unless you are in plain view of parents. Make sure that they can access your passwords all the time. Ask to have proper safety nets put in place on the computer, television, or any other electronic venues. Once those images have become part of your mind, it will affect you for a long time. I have heard men say that years later they can still see those first pictures that they found unsuspectingly. Keeping yourself pure is hard work, but it will pay rich dividends in the end. You cannot put enough safeguards in this area. Do so with all diligence.

I would also warn about the movies that you attend. They often make issues of sin seem so harmless. They are not. Read movie reviews such as the ones that are on Focus on the Family's web site and be informed. Small scenes may seem insignificant, but they are not. Sin does have its pleasure, but you, along with Moses, must resist these pleasures for a loftier goal. God will reward you deeply for such godly thinking and walking.

Don't Keep Things from Your Parents

Sometimes things happen and you believe it necessary to keep your parents out of the loop. There are a myriad of reasons why this may seem like a good idea at the time, but I am not sure there is ever a good

I Heart Parenting

reason. Parents have been given to you for your protection and you need to utilize their wisdom often. Keeping them from information is keeping you from the first line of defense for your overall protection. It's like playing a contact sport without any protective gear. Injuries are almost guaranteed. Secrets from Mom and Dad are unwise and unfruitful.

I realize that there might be a time where you believe that if your parents knew, they would be heartbroken. They might, but they will be far more heartbroken by the fact that you could not trust them with this sensitive information. That will crush their hearts in a much deeper way. Not giving the information to your parents is, in a sense, being dishonest. Lying to Mom and Dad is a path you never want to travel.

I am sure that someone will come up with a unique situation that requires keeping something from their parents. Of course I am not talking about the surprise 25th wedding anniversary like our children kept from us. I am referring to that which parents need to know about. It's not very often that a parent wishes you hadn't told them something! If you are in doubt, discuss the situation with the parent who you think will be most rational and careful with the information. But don't withhold things from your parents. You will be blessed by the communication, and so will they.

Don't Allow Peer Pressure to Control You

Some children are followers and some children are leaders. The same goes for them when they become adults. Children who are natural leaders grow up to be leaders. Children who are followers grow up to be those who follow. There is nothing wrong with being a follower or a leader. Much of this is how God has wired you. But there is something important about each of these that should not go unnoticed.

First, if you are called to be a leader, make sure you lead well. Leadership is a gift to you from God, and you don't want to abuse it nor neglect it. I have seen natural leaders who have used their ability to help others go down a bad path. How sad. Leaders then use peer pressure to force the cautious into behaviors that they do not want to do. Abuse of leadership gifts happens all the time, but teen leaders especially need to avoid this.

Second, if you are a natural follower, don't let someone with leadership gifts and persuasive talk lead you into mischief or sin. Many young people have succumbed to peer pressure and have given in to do that which normally they would not. Be willing to stand, even if that means standing alone. Be willing to be different. Peer pressure has caused many innocent young people to do things that they would never normally be willing to do. Avoid joining up with the crowd and going with the cool group. Will they be there to help pick up the pieces if you end up on the wrong side of peer pressure? Of course not. Peer pressure should never be used to cause someone to do something that they don't want to do, yet it happens all the time. Don't become another statistic.

Use your peer pressure in a positive way. "Hey, we are all going to youth group tonight. Come on!" "Hey, we are doing a small group Bible study; grab a Bible!" "Uh oh, you say you're a Christian; would God want you to do this?" Positive peer pressure has much better results than negative peer pressure!

Watch Your Mouth and Be Respectful

It is alarming today to hear how kids talk to their parents or other adults. If my generation had talked back to their parents the way the kids talk to their parents today, many would not have survived! It is disrespectful and shameful to hear how kids talk to their parents. And this holds true even in some Christian homes.

Many television shows and movies endorse such behavior. Some of the coolest kids are those who have a sharp tongue. They can cut and slice and dice a person in a heartbeat. They can cut you down while everyone laughs. Whatever kid can throw out the meanest and nastiest comments is usually considered the coolest. If they speak that way to their parents, they get bonus points with their friends.

For Christian children this ought not to be. In fact, it should be the exact opposite! Scripture says we should speak to one another respectfully and treat parents with extra respect. Try to put yourself in your parents' shoes. Would you want your children to speak to you in that manner? By the way, I have seen where these things do come back to haunt you. Children who obey and honor their parents seem to have children that do the same. Children who disobey and disrespect their parents seem to have children that disobey and disrespect them. It is not just a coincidence, because Scripture says that we reap what we sow.

Youth tend to focus on the outside. I heard recently that the number one graduation gift for girls has been plastic surgery. Really? Plastic surgery? If you make idols of sports figures and Hollywood icons, you'll stay focused on stuff that fades. Here's a news flash: beauty doesn't last. But the heart lasts forever! And that is what God looks at. It can grow deeper and stronger and more beautiful every day. The outside cannot do anything but fade and decay. How much money do you spend (or want to spend) on the trendy clothes, the special hair dos, the latest makeup, the expensive purses, shoes, etc. It is all about the style and fitting in with the crowd. I am not saying that you should never buy trendy clothes or try to fit in to some level. The point I am trying to make is that these things are not lasting, and overall, they aren't particularly important. Over the years I have met some beautiful people who, outwardly, were not necessarily the most stylish or most physically attractive. Yet they were so beautiful inside that you really did not notice the outside. I have also met quite a few beautiful and very stylish young people who were so full of themselves that they were not very attractive at all. Now I don't have a problem with someone being beautiful both on the outside and inside, but far too much attention is given to that which is not going to last. Make every effort to ensure that you are radiating beauty from the inside so that they will notice the beauty and be drawn to the One who is making us like Himself, the Beautiful One.

Understand that You Don't Have All the Answers

You are not as smart as you think. Many teens and young adults in this self-absorbed society think they are smarter than anyone else around them—their teachers, youth leaders, and of course, their parents. Now not every youth would say such a thing, but you can tell by how hard it is for them to ever receive advice or counsel. Think of how many times you have heard some adult tell you something and it has literally gone in one ear and come out of the other. Many parents have just thrown up their hands and concluded that it is a hopeless case. Are you really that hopeless? Of course not. If parents aren't quite as dumb as we think, then we need to consider the idea that we might just be slightly dumber than we might believe.

The wisdom of the older generation can often get lost in the arrogance of the younger generation. I realize that not all older people are wise, but many of their experiences and much wisdom is lost because we don't even ask to see what's there! Do you listen to the stories and advice of your parents and grandparents, or do you roll your eyes and sigh and wonder when they will be done talking?

My point is that you need to be teachable and remain teachable. Adults have to do this, too! Learn, learn, and after you have learned, learn some more. Put an emphasis on listening and paying close attention. God has given you two ears and one mouth, so use the ears twice as much.

I remember growing up and hearing the phrase "Children should be seen and not heard." That is actually not a bad phrase. A little extreme, maybe. But unfortunately, the pendulum has swung the other way. Try this: the next time you have a conversation with Mom or Dad, try to listen every time they speak, without even planning what you're going to say or thinking of something else. Be sure you understand what they are saying before you respond. Be as teachable as possible. If nothing else, it will surprise your parents! It will also show your respect, and if your parents know you respect them and are teachable, they will be a lot less likely to nag you! They know you've heard, understood, and applied their advice the first time, so they won't need to say it again.

You want your parents to be patient with you, as well as they should, but you also need to be patient with them. They are not perfect. They are going to make mistakes. Learn to forgive them for making a mistake and learn to let it go. Hanging on to the past mistakes will only cause long-term pain and consequences. You are not hurting them by holding on to a grudge. You are truly hurting yourself.

Yes, your parents will do wrong. Yes, they will treat you unfairly at times. Yes, you will be disciplined for something you did not do. You might have some pain at times for things that are unfair. Don't live in the past. The past is what it is. To continue to hold on to the past and the pain is only hurting yourself. Learn to let it go, before hanging onto old hurts and grudges becomes a habit. Too many adults today are in some kind of therapy or counseling over their childhood. Learn to forgive now so bitterness will not settle in and become destructive in your adult life. What a waste that would be!

Buck that Trend of Church Departure

Nearly every book you read today about the youth and the present culture includes some statistics about youth leaving the church. It saddens me that the statistics are so high, but one is far too many. There seems to be a trend that once you are college age, you are on your own and can begin to make your own decisions. I would challenge you to defend that in the Bible! You are on your own when your parents give you that blessing. Until then, you are under your parents' authority and need to be obeying and honoring them. It is disrespectful to do otherwise.

If you stay at home and go to community college, continue to attend church with your parents and be involved. Don't just sit there and soak and sour. Children often think it is right that they find some church other than their parents' church. They may have been raised in this church, baptized, and taught for all their years, but now that they are wiser than their parents, they need a different church. How sad. I have discovered that it is not about a different church, but about avoiding being under authority. There is little to no accountability in this change, you feel free to come and go as you please. Besides, you're exercising your faith and making independent decisions, right? And Mom and Dad ought to be happy that you are going to church, shouldn't they? I have found that most young people who take this path of leaving their parent's church tend to drift for years, and many never return. Stay with your parent's church. It will actually affirm your parents more than you realize.

Now there might be the need to switch a church at this time. I am not going to say that it should never happen, but it ought to be for very definite spiritual reasons, such as: immorality in the church, false teaching, or something of this level. Just leaving because another church has a better music program or more kids your age does not make leaving a wise decision. I remember several occasions where young adults stayed at a church even though the numbers were small. Some people counseled them go to a larger church if they expected to find a Christian mate. You mean God can only bring a mate to someone in a larger church? Wow, God is more limited than I thought! Their "advisors" were quite surprised when both of these young people found mates right in their own church!

Another area where young people drift is when they go off to college. One of the first things your parents ought to do is help you find a good church. Also, you should attend faithfully and become involved in ministry there. Start taking ownership of your faith with an aggressive act of commitment and service. Then give regular reports to your parents of your faithfulness and activity. Summers also ought to be spent being active and committed to a local church. You may also want to use this time to serve in some kind of mission ministry. During my summers between my college years, I was blessed to work at a Christian camp. That camp eventually was the means of my first employment out of college. I wonder how I would have found that job had I not have been active serving during the summers between my college years. God rewards faithful service. He does not reward slothfulness. Scripture even commends singles to use their unmarried years to serve faithfully since they have no marriage ties to constrain them. Far too many singles waste their single years doing little for the Savior. These are wasted years that you can never get back. Serve and watch God bless.

Sometimes, you graduate from college and return home. I believe it is wise not to get an apartment and separate from family at this time. If Mom and Dad can house you, you should live there. And the same that has been said before still holds true: get involved in the church where your parents attend and support their godly leadership and example. If your parents, who are still in authority over you, believe that this church is a good church, then you need to attend with them. How said to watch as children leave the church of their parents as if they know more about God's leading than their parents. Don't become another statistic. The same holds true when you get married. There is nothing more special than watching families begin to set up the standard of generational faith in a local church. Stop looking elsewhere and show support to the godly leading of your parents.

Keep a Close Walk with the Lord

One final thought that I want to challenge you with is your personal walk with the Lord. Do not let the years of your youth go by without cultivating a devotional life, prayer life, and servant's heart. Take discipleship seriously as a youth and you will mature into a real man or woman of God.

The world needs to see God-fearing men and women. And it starts not after college, but during your childhood. Learning to walk close to the Savior will grow and mature you into a God-fearing adult who can deal with the hard things: pain, frustration, and even life's tragedies. Don't wait until you grow up. Devotion to God today, first and foremost, will prepare you for all your tomorrows. Will you accept the challenge?

Part Four

The Conclusion of It All

What will you leave behind?

18

Leaving a Legacy

BEFORE I SHARE MY heart with you in this section, let me explain what I mean by leaving a legacy. There are two components to a legacy. There is the impact that we have on one another that is imprinted in each life. It comprises imprints such as how we view life, how we face obstacles, what we believe is important, and other critical thoughts like that. The other component is what those whom we leave behind think of us and how we impacted them. What is said at a funeral eulogy may not be accurate, but what people think about you shapes future generations. Don't take lightly what others believe about you after you are gone. Those beliefs shape the future generations more than you may know.

Whether you like it or not, you are going to leave some kind of legacy. The question is "what kind of a legacy?" We are all products of many components, but we cannot underestimate the importance of parental influence. How many children have said that they would never be like their parents, only to find out years later that they are a lot like their parents? I remember watching television with my dad. He had an uncanny ability to predict the story before it ever unfolded. I am not sure how he was able to do so, but it so aggravated me that I found myself often leaving the room in disgust. "Thanks, Dad, for ruining another show for me! I can't wait until I am a parent because I would never do that to my children!" Fast forward to watching television in our house today, and guess what? For some reason, I cannot resist the temptation to do the same. (Now I have learned to control it somewhat after extensive fussing from my family.) We really do replicate the parenting styles, values, and opinions that have been passed down to us. So, be careful how you raise your children, because they are going to model what they see.

In the parenting legacy, there is the truth that our children will learn from us the things which we hope we won't pass down to them. They will learn to model our language, habits, behaviors, and anything that could later develop into that which is not well pleasing in His sight. But that is not the direction that I want to go with this last chapter. Yes, we all know that unfortunately we may just leave behind some of our sinful behavior and attitudes. We can only fall on the grace of God and beg Him to remove as much as possible of the sin that we have left behind.

But I want to talk about something far greater than the bad, and that is the beauty and blessing of a legacy made after the heart of God. I would like us to focus on the opportunity that we have to truly make an earthly difference for the Kingdom. Just think of it in terms of how the impact is great with the picture of the family. It is not just you in this view. There are the two parents and the children. Let's just suppose that there are two children in the family. You individually have doubled your chance of making a difference in this world. And although there are many influences on a child, we can choose to be the major influence in their lives for the cause of Christ. It is the whole concept of discipleship that Jesus talked about and that He passed on to others. Matthew 28:19–20 and 2 Timothy 2:2 mention this exact philosophy of ministry. The same concept that Jesus taught His disciples is the concept that I want to reiterate to you. You are not just raising a child to be on his/her own. You are helping change the world for the cause of Christ. Your children need to be taught that this world is not about them, but about Him. We have been bought with a price, now we need to glorify God in our bodies, which are His.

So, how do we go about creating a legacy that will last far beyond our years? First, we need to realize that there will be a legacy whether we want it to be or not. I do funerals all the time, and over the years I have learned to leave the eulogy (the family legacy) up to the loved ones. I really couldn't care less about what a family member says about their dear departed loved one. They always say that grandpa is in a better place, even if the guy was a true heathen. I don't give eulogies because I will not commit them to Heaven if they have not had a personal saving encounter with Jesus. So, the "legacy" is given by the family. I then proceed to drive home scripturally how someone can go to Heaven when they die and know for sure that they are on their way as they are alive.

Leaving a Legacy

But either intentionally or unintentionally, every parent who dies is going to leave behind a legacy.

My sister-in-law, Lara Webster, was taken from us via a brain tumor when she was 39. She left behind my brother and their three children. No one saw this coming. She seemed healthy and vivacious, and for all intents and purposes, and seemed prepared to raise her children for their entire lives. But God had other plans, much to our dismay. We buried her on a cold winter's day with several feet of snow all around. It was a private burial for just family and a few close friends. At a later memorial service, my brother, Tim, who is also a pastor, led the service. On that night we heard of the legacy of Lara Webster. Not only had she poured her life into her children, she had also poured her life into many others. They kept coming up one by one and giving that testimony. Lara had decided long ago that the privilege to be on this earth was not about her. She was here for Kingdom business and to raise her children with that mindset. Just yesterday Tim and his children were at my house. As I sat and talked with Mark, the youngest child, he told me a story that certainly begins to paint the picture of the upcoming legacy. He is on a basketball team. They had lost their most recent game, but what happened afterwards was the key. Mark was disgusted by some of the language of his teammates, and he told them so. He was already learning to be part of a legacy Lara left behind. She had passed on that legacy to him and he was accepting the challenge. That is just one small portion of a story that will continue to unfold in the years to come as the kids remember their mom and what she taught them.

Now I want to reflect on the legacy that has been left to me by my family. Now I don't want to give the impression that my family was perfect while I was growing up, because it was not. But I see no need to point out the flaws. The concern in this section is to remind the reader of how a legacy can truly be passed along in a positive way.

My grandparents were highly influential in my life. My grandfather loved to lead in the worship. His father was a lay leader, and he passed that along to my grandfather, and today I am a pastor. My grandmother had a passion for missions and pastors. She loved every pastor she ever met, and I never ever heard her complain or deride a pastor. She passed on her love for mission work, and my brothers and I go regularly all over the world on mission trips. She was the mission's committee chairperson and personally gave much to missions. She also loved to read great books and now I have a library that is full of classics and new great works. My grandmother, whom I called Mom, was a woman of prayer. We lived just two houses down from her, and I would often on Saturday mornings, or any day during the summer, go and visit. If Pop (my grandfather) was not home, I went in to see Mom. I remember that on one occasion, as I walked into their house, I heard a noise coming from the family room. I heard the words, but I was not sure what I was hearing. I crept around the corner and saw my grandmother kneeling with her face in the Bible and crying and weeping before God. It truly left an amazing impression on my little mind, especially when I saw it happen frequently as the years went on. The importance of prayer was left as a legacy for me.

My parents also are part of that legacy. One component of their legacy in particular was my mother's consistency in parenting. When she said that there was no dessert because I did not eat my dinner, begging changed nothing. When she said I did not clean up my room and therefore could not go somewhere, she kept true to her word. But not only was she consistent in what she said, she was also consistent in how she lived. I never saw her waiver in her faith or her walk. Consistency was modeled for me daily. Another time she modeled for me was in the area of forgiving others. For example, a certain man had wronged our family. One night when we were out to dinner, my mom went over to this young man and hugged him and told him she loved him. He had wronged our family, but there was no reason not to love him. God's Word says we are to love our enemies. It was a legacy that will linger for a long time. And this was not the only time she modeled it for me. She was an amazing example of forgiveness.

My father also left a legacy for me. He spent many hours selflessly giving to others. He did not have much money, but he had time. He would leave work and care for the widows in our town. There were several black families also that lived in our community that my dad personally ministered to. I think that he was the only white man to ever enter those homes. There was also a black community about three miles from our house, and a certain man in that community had a general store, somewhat similar to Dad's. This man, however, was blind. My dad supplied his store with anything he needed at cost. Dad made no money off of this man, but cared for him as if he were a family member. I learned from Dad years ago that color is never the issue, it is always the heart. Thankfully, our church has learned from my dad as well, passing along the legacy. Recently, our church leadership voted a young couple as the youth pastor and wife for our church. We are a predominantly white church in a predominantly white community. Not much we can do about that. So, what does the youth pastor have to do with our discussion? The youth pastor is a young black man married to a white woman. They love the Lord and are a great couple. Again, I certainly don't want to give the impression that my parents or grandparents were perfect. They were not and neither will we be. But they passed down a Kingdom legacy consistently throughout their lives.

Church attendance was one of the biggest legacies that my parents, grandparents, and aunt and uncle left me. The little country church was down the street from our houses, not more than 500 yards. Our three families faithfully attended church, and when I say faithfully, I mean nothing but a hurricane kept them away. We were there Sunday morning, Sunday evening, Wednesday, and every other time the church was open for business. If the church doors were open, we were there, no questions asked. I never ever heard my family asking "Are we going to church tonight?" The answer would have been, "Are you breathing?" I saw my parents actively work in the church. They taught Sunday school, Vacation Bible School, and wherever else was needed. I saw them regularly read the Scriptures, and we often had family devotions. The Word and church were as natural to my family as eating. It did not cause me to retreat from God, but to draw near. Why do we think that if we saturate our children with God and church and Scripture that they are going to turn away from it? My family intentionally and purposefully gave me Jesus on a regular basis and I learned to love Him with my whole heart. Now, was I always on the right course? No, but the overall saturation took deep root in my heart and I believe that much of what I am today I owe to the legacy left by my family.

What will your legacy be? Will you leave behind a legacy that you were a great fisherman? Nobody caught the fish that you did. Will you leave behind that you were a great hunter? Trophies of all kinds hang on your walls. Will you leave behind the knowledge that you were a shrewd businessman, or that you had lots of friends? Will you leave behind that which is temporal and fleeting, or will you leave behind that which is about the Kingdom?

I want to challenge you to go after the hearts of your children and determine that what you will leave behind in your children will be a lasting legacy for the cause of Christ. Your children ought to remember the most important things about you; that is, how you invested in them for the eternal things of God. The hours you spend with your children cannot be retrieved. If you leave this earth and have only prepared them for the earthly, you have missed a great opportunity to make a difference for Him. "Choose you this day whom you will serve..." Joshua challenged Israel (Jos 24:15), "As for me and my house, we will serve the Lord."

Afterword

ONE OF THE CHALLENGES of writing a book versus teaching in front of a live audience is that the author does not get a chance to clarify anything that may have come across ambiguously. Let me begin by offering my humblest apology for any teaching that was hard to follow or inapplicable for your situation. I have tried to share my heart with you because I have a great love for children. My deepest desire is to honor God and help parents do their best to train up a generation of God-fearing children.

Ever since my first year of Bible college, I have participated in some form of youth ministry. I worked at a teen camp for several years. During Bible college, I taught Sunday school at a nearby army base. After college, I taught middle and high school kids, while also coaching and being an active part of their lives. Then I went on to seminary and taught in the Bible college and coached the basketball team. During my last year of seminary, I was hired to be the youth pastor of an inner-city church. After Bible college, God led me to a church that had a Christian school. This doesn't mean that I have been a great youth worker and have all the answers. But God gave me a heart for the youth in my early years, and over time he placed me in those positions so I could experience their needs. My prayer is that this book will have an impact for the children and their families.

I don't expect my readers to agree with all that I have written. All I ask is that you contemplate what I have shared with you, and that you would prayerfully consider these thoughts and principles. I have not written them carelessly, and my prayer is that you would not consider them carelessly. I hope that it helps you make an eternal impact on your kids for the glory of God. May you take this book and pass it on, and may one day these humble hands lay it all at the feet of Jesus.

Bibliography

"Add Health." UNC Carolina Population Center. http://www.cpc.unc.edu/projects/addhealth (accessed July 22, 2012).

"Alcoholism - The Alcoholism Home Page." http://alcoholism.about.com (accessed July 22, 2012).

America's children: key national indicators of well-being, 2007. 10th anniversary ed. Washington, D.C.: Federal Interagency Forum on Child and Family Statistics, 2007.

Associated Press. "Movie Ticket Sales Fell Sharply in 2011." CBS News. http://www.cbsnews.com (accessed July 22, 2012).

Bolding, Joshua. "Church Donations Growing at Less than Half the Rate of Overall Charitable Giving." *Deseret News*, January 20, 2012. http://www.deseretnews.com/article/700217384/Church-donations-growing-at-less-than-half-the-rate-of-overall-charitable-giving.html?pg=all (accessed June 22, 2012).

"CDC Features - 2011 Youth Risk Behavior Survey (YRBS) Results." Centers for Disease Control and Prevention. http://www.cdc.gov/Features/YRBS (accessed July 22, 2012).

"Children and Divorce: Statistics." Children and Divorce: Information, tips and real life stories for parents. http://children-and-divorce.com (accessed June 25, 2012).

"Eating Disorders and Kids: Statistics Show How Little We Know." GoodTherapy.org. http://www.goodtherapy.org (accessed July 22, 2012).

Hamm, Ken, Britt Beamer, Todd Hillard. *Already Gone: Why your kids will quit church and what you can do to stop it.* Green Springs: Master Books, 2009.

MacArthur, John. *Safe in the Arms of God: Words from Heaven About the Death of a Child.* Nashville: Thomas Nelson Publishers, 2003.

Meeker, Margaret J. *Epidemic: how teen sex is killing our kids.* Washington, DC: LifeLine Press, 2002.

Minino, AM, SL Murphy, J Xu, and KD Kochanek. "Deaths: Final Data for 2008." *National Vital Statistics Reports* 59, no. 10 (2011): 1. http://www.cdc.gov/nchs/data/nvsr/nvsr59/nvsr59_10.pdf (accessed June 22, 2012).

Rai, Anund. "Money Spent on Gaming to Reach $112 Billion in 2015: Gartner." vcircle.com. http://techcircle.vcircle.com (accessed July 23, 2012).

Rector, Robert, Kirk Johnson, and Lauren Noyes. "Sexually Active Teenagers Are More Likely to Be Depressed and Attempt Suicide." Conservative Policy Research and Analysis. http://www.heritage.org (accessed July 22, 2012).

"Resources." The Council on Alcohol & Drug Abuse. http://www.gdcada.org/Resources.aspx (accessed July 22, 2012).

"Sex and America's Teenagers," Guttmacher Institute: Adolescents. http://www.guttmacher.org/sections/adolescents.php (accessed July 22, 2012).

Watson, G.D. *Tract #76.* Grand Rapids, MI: Faith, Prayer, & Tract League, 1924.

www.ingramcontent.com/pod-product-compliance
Lightning Source LLC
Chambersburg PA
CBHW071446150426
43191CB00008B/1251